Snacks 6

Appetizers 16

Salads and Sides 26

Main Courses 48

Desserts 88

Glossary 106

References 110

Dedicated to everyone who has already realized that taking care of your brain is as important as taking care of your body.

Posit Science - http://www.PositScience.com

Steven Aldrich
CEO, Posit Science
@PositScience

Dear Reader,

At Posit Science, we build clinically proven brain fitness programs so people can give their brains the best, most effective workouts possible. The benefits of challenging your brain with our products have been demonstrated in over 60 published studies of our technology. Our programs speed up and sharpen key brain functions, so that the brain can operate as smoothly and efficiently as possible. The result: faster thinking, sharper focus, and better memory.

We know, however, that brain training is just one piece of the puzzle. Diet, physical exercise, social activities, new learning, and meditation can all play a role in creating and sustaining brain fitness.

In this cookbook, we've chosen to highlight how what you eat affects brain fitness. But since we're not chefs ourselves, we asked for help from the global food blogging community in creating the recipes. We hope you enjoy them!

One important note: The science of brain-healthy eating is not (yet) definitive. It's more suggestive than conclusive. Some of the ingredients we've included here have quite a bit of evidence behind them (such as fatty fish), while others are more controversial (such as açaí). We've only put forward foods that have at least some evidence for brain-healthy benefits—but what gets included on the list of "brain foods" may well change as more information becomes available. As we learn more, we'll provide updated information at www.thinkfoodcookbook.com.

By using the recipes in this cookbook, you are a part of a movement that is making brain fitness as important to our society as physical fitness. Here's to good food—and a healthy brain!

*Flaxseed

A superfood chock-full of omega-3 fatty acids, vitamin B6, and lignans, flaxseed has great potential for improving brain health and function. But make sure to eat it ground...whole seeds don't deliver the nutrients as well.

Get the facts - pg. 106

Flaxseed Grissini

About the blogger

Wild Yeast - http://www.wildyeastblog.com

Susan Tenney
@wildyeast

Bread is exciting to Susan because it is virtually synonymous with food itself: it's infinitely versatile and varied, everyone likes it, every cuisine includes it, and no meal is complete without it. Baking bread engages and satisfies every one of her senses in a way that nothing else does, and blogging about it on Wild Yeast is like breaking bread with friends all over the world. A graduate of the San Francisco Baking Institute's professional bread and pastry program, Susan remains most interested in figuring out how to pull bakery-quality breads from her home oven, and helping others learn how to do so. When she is not baking, she masquerades as a family nurse practitioner.

Flaxseed Grissini

Serves 24

Dough Ingredients

1 cup + 2 Tbsps (150 g) all-purpose or bread flour

⅔ cup (149 g) cold water

3 Tbsps (23 g) rye or whole wheat flour

½ cup ground flaxseeds (flax meal)

Scant ¾ tsp (2.3 g) instant yeast

¾ tsp salt

2¼ tsps olive oil

Topping Suggestions

Coarse salt

Coarsely-ground pepper

Whole flaxseeds

Whole or coarsely chopped fennel seeds

Sesame seeds

Coarse semolina

1. In the bowl of a food processor with the metal blade, combine the flour, rye flour, flaxseed, salt, and yeast. Pulse to combine.

2. In a liquid measuring cup, combine 2/3 cup (149 grams) of cold water with the olive oil. With the food processor running, add the liquids to the dry ingredients in a thin stream.

3. Continue processing until the dough more or less holds together (it will not form a ball because it is too sticky at this point), and for about 30 seconds beyond that. The total processing time should be about 90 seconds.

4. Transfer the dough to a lightly oiled, covered container.

5. Let rise at room temperature until the dough doubles in volume, about one hour.

6. Preheat the oven to 350 degrees F and line two baking sheets with parchment paper.

7. Divide the dough into two pieces. While working with the first piece, cover and refrigerate the other.

8. On a lightly floured counter, pat the dough into a rectangle of roughly 8 x 4 inches.

9. Sprinkle the dough evenly with your choice of topping(s).

10. With a pizza cutter or chef's knife, cut the dough into 12 strips.

11. On a flour-free section of counter, roll each dough strip into a snake the length of your baking sheet. Space them evenly across the sheet.

12. Spray or brush the grissini lightly with olive oil.

13. Bake for 25–30 minutes, until well browned.

14. Cool on a wire rack.

Pecan, Cranberry & Orange Muffins

Pecan, Cranberry & Orange Muffins

Makes 12 muffins

½ cup + 2 Tbsps all-purpose flour

½ cup + 2 Tbsps whole wheat flour

1 Tbsp baking powder

⅓ cup superfine sugar
   (also known as caster sugar)

¼ cup pecans, roughly chopped

Zest of ½ orange

1 egg

¾ cup milk

½ stick butter, melted

2 tsp orange juice

½ cup cranberries

1. Preheat your oven to 425 degrees F. Line a 12 cup muffin pan with paper liners.

2. Sift the two flours and baking powder into a large mixing bowl, then stir in sugar, pecans, and orange zest.

3. In a small mixing bowl, beat together the egg, milk, melted butter, and orange juice.

4. Add the wet ingredients to the dry and beat with a wooden spoon until just combined.

5. Add the cranberries and stir briefly. (Do not overmix or the muffins will be tough.)

6. Spoon the batter into the prepared muffin liners, filling to around 2/3 full. Bake in the oven for 20 minutes or until the domes are lightly golden and firm to the touch.

7. Remove muffins from oven. Allow to cool slightly, and serve while still warm.

*Cranberry

Cranberries have been identified as an excellent dietary source of high-quality antioxidants, which have been shown to help maintain healthy cognitive functioning. Scientists continue to study berries and antioxidants to learn more about potential brain benefits.

Get the facts - pg. 106

About the blogger

Katiecakes - http://iheartkatiecakes.blogspot.com

Kate Deacon
@Katie_Cakes

Katie is a little lassie from Newcastle, in the Northeast of England. She has a passion for all things sweet and an intense ache to bake. Be it as simple as a cupcake or as delicate as a French macaron, she is always ready to whip on an apron and give it her all. Her adoration of all things baked sprung from lost evenings trawling the internet, daydreaming over the hundreds of baking blogs that flashed upon her screen. One day it finally struck her to get her head out of the clouds and start her own. Katiecakes was the brain child of that moment of epiphany. Two years later Katie is still baking and even running her own cupcake company which supplies the Northeast with sugary sweetness.

Fruited Granola

Fruited Granola

Serves 8

5½ cups traditional rolled oats
  (not instant)

1 tsp ground cinnamon

1 tsp ground ginger

¾ tsp salt

¾ cup light brown sugar

¾ cup applesauce

¼ cup honey

1½ cups almonds, chopped

¾ cup dried cranberries

¾ cup dried apricots, chopped

1. Preheat the oven to 325 degrees F. Line a large baking sheet with parchment paper.

2. In a large bowl, mix together the oats, cinnamon, ginger and salt.

3. In a medium bowl, whisk together the brown sugar, applesauce, and honey until thoroughly combined.

4. Add the wet ingredients to the dry ingredients, along with the chopped almonds. Mix well, until all of the oats are moistened. Spread on prepared pan in an even layer.

5. Bake for 30 minutes, then remove the pan from the oven and turn the granola over very carefully using a wide spatula. Return to the oven and bake for an additional 10–15 minutes, or until crisp and golden.

6. Cool completely on the baking sheet.

7. Break up the granola into chunks and stir in the dried fruit. Store in an airtight container.

*Oats

Fiber-rich oats provide a steady supply of energy to the brain, which may improve learning. They are also rich in selenium, an antioxidant that has been shown to have protective effects in a variety of brain disorders and age-related cognitive problems.

Get the facts - pg. 106

About the blogger

Brown Eyed Baker - http://www.browneyedbaker.com

Michelle Norris
@browneyedbaker

Michelle has been baking since she was a teenager, and has a soft spot for rich, decadent desserts. It's one of the main reasons that her food blog is almost exclusively dedicated to sweets. However, she believes in balance and while she loves flourless chocolate tortes and tall cheesecakes, she says she knows that she can't eat them for every meal. Michelle's rule of thumb is to strive to eat wholesome and balanced foods about 80% of the time. She credits that philosophy with keeping her healthy and enabling her to indulge a bit when the urge strikes. She loves being able to use her food blog as a way to share her love of food and to encourage others to become more comfortable and confident in the kitchen.

Blueberry-nana Smoothie

Blueberry-nana Smoothie

Serves 1

1 cup milk

½ cup frozen blueberries

1 banana

1 Tbsp coconut oil

2 tsps flaxseed oil

4-5 ice cubes

1. Combine milk, blueberries, banana, coconut oil, and flaxseed oil in a blender or smoothie cup, fitted with an immersion blender.

2. Add ice cubes and blend until desired consistency.

3. Pour into a glass and enjoy immediately.

***Blueberries**

Among the general public, blueberries might be the most widely recognized "brain food" around. They are powerful antioxidants and anti-inflammatories, making them popular subjects for studies on cognitive health.

Get the facts - pg. 106

About the blogger

Food Loves Writing - http://foodloveswriting.com

Photo Courtesy Rebecca Brogan
Shannalee T'Koy
@foodloves

At Food Loves Writing, Shannalee T'Koy talks about food to talk about everything else, from Chicago weather to the value of relationships to the great things like faith, hope and love. She started her literary food blog back in August 2008, on the anniversary of the day her grandma, the woman who taught her to bake, passed away. Since then, it has become a place for discovery, for mistakes, for embracing every day she's been given; she also thinks its become a place her grandma would have liked.

Amy's Cinnamon Almonds

Amy's Cinnamon Almonds

Serves 16

1 lb almonds

1 egg white

1 tsp vanilla

¾ cup brown sugar

¼ cup white sugar

½ tsp salt

2 tsps cinnamon

1. Preheat the oven to 225 degrees F.

2. Whisk the egg white and vanilla until fluffy.

3. Stir almonds into the egg white mixture.

4. In separate bowl combine the sugars, salt and cinnamon.

5. Pour the almonds into the sugar mixture and mix to coat the almonds with the sugar.

6. Pour almonds onto a cookie sheet and spread into a thin layer. Bake for 1 hour, stirring every 15 minutes.

7. Let cool and eat.

*Almonds

Almonds are one of the most concentrated sources of vitamin E available, and vitamin E at a high daily dose has been shown to delay the progression of Alzheimer's disease.

Get the facts - pg. 106

About the blogger

Super Healthy Kids - http://blog.superhealthykids.com

Amy Roskelley
@healthykids

Amy is a mother of three kids and a graduate of Health Education, and she loves food. She is passionate about teaching children that healthy food not only can taste great, but also make you feel great! The purpose of Amy's blog is to give parents the tools they need to feed their children the best meals they can.

Sesame

Sesame seeds contain lipophilic antioxidants, which may prevent age-related diseases. Adding sesame seeds and other small but high-impact brain foods (like flaxseed and turmeric) to your dishes is a simple, tasty way to put a little brain boost in every bite.

Get the facts - pg. 106

Salted Sesame Brittle

About the blogger

Anne's Food - http://annesfood.blogspot.com

Anne Skoogh
@annesfood

Anne thinks that life is much too short to eat just because you're hungry. Everyone should take the time–not that it takes much–to cook and eat things that are both good for you and delicious. It's not difficult; everyone can do it! If Anne has one mission with her blog, it's to inspire courage to cook. Everyone can be a great cook, no matter their previous experience or the size of their kitchens.

Try making a quick risotto for a weeknight dinner, or a stew that basically makes itself while you're free to read a book or take a walk! You'll be hooked in no time!

Smoked Salmon Canapé with Sesame Brittle

Serves 4

1¾ oz smoked wild salmon,
   cut into small strips

⅓ cup fennel, thinly sliced

5 whole strawberries, diced

1 tsp white wine vinegar

1 tsp canola oil

1 tsp Sichuan peppercorns,
   crushed (can substitute
   pink peppercorns)

Salted Sesame Brittle

½ cup sugar

⅓ cup honey

1 Tbsp salted butter

¾ cup toasted sesame seeds

Flaky sea salt to taste

1. Combine salmon, fennel, and strawberries in a bowl.

2. Add vinegar and oil and mix to combine. Season with crushed peppercorns and mix again.

3. Move to plates or serving dish and garnish with fennel fronds and sesame brittle (recipe follows.)

Salted Sesame Brittle

1. Prepare a baking sheet with a Silpat baking mat or greased parchment paper and set aside.

2. In a medium pot, bring sugar and honey to a boil, stirring constantly. When mixture begins to boil, stop stirring and allow it to continue boiling undisturbed until it turns a medium gold color. (Watch very closely, as once the color starts changing it will darken quickly.)

3. Remove pot from heat and stir in butter and sesame seeds. Pour onto a baking sheet lined with aTeflon or Silpat baking mat.

4. Put a second Silpat or greased parchment on top of hot mixture and use a rolling pin to roll it out as thinly as possible.

5. Uncover, sprinkle with flaky sea salt, and let it cool completely before breaking into shards.

*Artichoke

Artichokes are rich in luteolin derivatives, a type of antioxidant flavonoid which has been shown to have positive effects on a wide variety of cognitive issues. Fun fact: the antioxidant value of an artichoke actually increases when the artichoke is fried! Of course, so do the calories...

Get the facts - pg. 106

Artichoke Ingredient

○ .... ○

About the blogger

La Note Restaurant - http://www.lanoterestaurant.com

Denise Ravizza

One of Denise's favorite childhood memories is enjoying fresh organic artichokes from the bush her grandfather planted on his ranch in Mill Valley, California, where the weather conditions are perfect for cultivating this amazing vegetable. It was here that her passion for cooking began and turned into a profession that she adores. As her career has blossomed, she has been fortunate to experience many endeavors, including testing the delicious recipes for the ThinkFood cookbook at La Note Restaurant in Berkeley, California. Enjoying locally grown organic ingredients fresh from the farm to the table is a tradition she cooks by. Here is an ode to the Reed Ranch.

Stuffed Artichokes with Gremolata & Greek Yogurt Dipping Sauce

Serves 4

4 whole artichokes

7 Tbsps olive oil, divided

1 onion, finely chopped

2 cloves garlic, minced

1¼ cup bread crumbs

Leaves from 4 sprigs fresh thyme

2 oz can roasted chili peppers, minced and drained

1 cup Parmesan cheese

Salt and pepper

Gremolata

¼ cup parsley, finely chopped

1 clove garlic, minced

1 tsp lemon zest

Dipping Sauce

½ cup Greek yogurt

½ cup sour cream

1. Trim the tough outer leaves of the artichokes and cut the top third off with a serrated knife. Cut the remaining prickly tips off with scissors. Cut the stem, close to the base, evenly so the artichoke stands up. Fill a large pot with one inch of water and place a steam basket inside with the artichokes in it. Cover and bring water to a boil. Steam the artichokes till the stems are knife tender, 30-40 minutes. With tongs, remove artichokes and set upside down on a paper napkin to drain any excess water. Let artichokes cool.

2. In a sauté pan over medium-low heat, add 2 tablespoons olive oil and onion and cook until onion starts to turn translucent, about 2 minutes. Add the garlic and thyme and cook one minute longer. Put onions and garlic in a bowl and add the bread crumbs, 1/2 cup Parmesan cheese, peppers, and salt and pepper to taste and stir to combine. Add the remaining 5 tablespoons of olive oil and stir until bread crumbs are moistened.

3. With a pairing knife remove the inside fuzzy leaves of the center of the artichoke, to create a small pocket for the filling, and gently spread out the outer leaves. Fill the center with the bread crumb filling and distribute it throughout the outer edges of the artichoke, gently pressing it in place. Let the artichoke sit in the fridge at least 4 hours or overnight for the filling to set.

Gremolata

1. In a small bowl, combine minced garlic, lemon zest and finely chopped parsley. Stir to combine.

Dipping Sauce

1. In a small bowl, combine the greek yogurt and sour cream. Stir to combine.

To Cook and Serve

1. Preheat broiler. Place the artichokes on a baking sheet and top with remaining 1/2 cup parmesan cheese. Broil the artichokes until the cheese and filling begin to brown (approximately 2-3 minutes).

2. Top each artichoke with gremolata and a dollop of the Greek yogurt dipping sauce on the side.

Perfect Butternut Squash Sage Dip

Perfect Butternut Squash Sage Dip

Serves 6-8

1 15 oz can butternut squash

4 heaping Tbsps garlic hummus

¼ cup maple syrup

1 tsp dried orange peel

2 Tbsps plain soy creamer

½ tsp sea salt

¼ tsp fresh black pepper

5 large fresh sage leaves,
  finely chopped

Cayenne and/or cinnamon,
  to taste (optional)

1. Spoon butternut squash puree into a small to medium mixing bowl.

2. Add hummus, maple syrup, soy creamer, orange peel, salt and pepper.

3. Mix well, until dip is smooth and well blended.

4. Fold in a pinch of sage leaves.

5. Microwave on high until dip is warm, about 1 minute.

6. Fold in remaining sage leaves and additional salt to taste, if desired. If adding cayenne and/or cinnamon, fold in to taste. Microwave for another 20 seconds then mix well again.

7. Spoon dip into a serving dish. Garnish with a whole sage leaf, if desired.

8. Serve dip lukewarm or at room temperature with crostini bread, crackers, or veggie sticks.

*Butternut Squash

Butternut squash is a winter squash that is rich in all kind of nutrients. It has several compounds that have brain-healthy potential: vitamins A and C, folic acid, and beta carotene, to name a few.

Get the facts - pg. 106

About the blogger

Healthy Happy Life - http://kblog.lunchboxbunch.com

Kathy Patalsky
@lunchboxbunch

Kathy grew up in Santa Cruz, California, where her passion for healthy vegan cooking and eating, food photography, green living and art began. Kathy received her B.S in Health Promotion from American University in Washington DC. She currently lives and eats in NYC with her foodie husband and their cat Nelly. As a self-taught vegan chef, she specializes in cuisine that is organic, vegan, and seasonal. Kathy's blog, Healthy. Happy. Life. features recipes, wellness tips, super foods, travel quips, and wellness news.

*Tomato

Dried tomatoes like those in this recipe have a higher concentration of lycopene than fresh or canned tomatoes. Lycopene may play a role in cognitive performance, especially in people with diabetes.

Get the facts - pg. 106

Sundried Tomato Ingredient

About the blogger

The Healthy Everythingtarian - http://www.thehealthyeverythingtarian.com

Holly Whittlef

Ever since Holly was a wee girl, she has always loved food. The taste, the smells, the sense of community, the love, the togetherness and the satisfaction of providing one of humankind's most innate needs—food was comfort. In turn, comfort also became food. Whether it was satisfying her saccharine sweet tooth with a bowl of cool, creamy ice cream or filling her plate with a yummy assortment of goods, food was Holly's friend. As Holly got older, she realized food could be her friend in a way that could make her healthier and more importantly, happier. Although Holly was never overweight, she realized she wasn't exactly treating her body as well as she should. Holly took action. She started researching more, learning more, eating fruits and vegetables more,

cooking more, creating recipes more. Before she knew it, food became a passion. If you asked her several years ago if she would be the author of a food blog, she probably would have laughed it off as a big, fat joke. But Holly is a blogger. And loves it. She loves constantly finding new ways to make healthy food taste delicious. And loves showing people that living a healthy life doesn't have to be boring or bland or devoid of dessert. On the contrary—it can be exciting, fun and include a daily dose of sweets! Living a happy, healthy life is one of the best things we can do for ourselves, and Holly feels privileged to be able to help people achieve just that every day.

Sundried Tomato and Goat Cheese Mini Quiches

Makes 12 mini quiches

1 sheet of frozen puff pastry

2 Tbsps olive oil

1 Tbsp garlic, minced

6 cups spinach leaves

3 oz sundried tomatoes packed in olive oil, drained and quartered

6 eggs

½ cup skim milk

1 tsp Italian seasoning

½ tsp salt

½ tsp crushed red pepper flakes

2 oz goat cheese, crumbled

Cooking spray

1. In a medium saucepan over medium-low heat, heat olive oil and sauté the garlic and spinach until the spinach is wilted. Remove from heat and let cool.

2. Meanwhile, in a medium-sized bowl, whisk together sundried tomatoes, eggs, milk, Italian seasoning, salt, and red pepper flakes. Add cooled spinach to the egg mixture and combine.

3. Carefully unfold thawed puff pastry sheet onto a lightly floured surface. Using a rolling pin, roll puff pastry to 1/8 inch thick.

4. Using a pizza cutter or knife, cut the pastry into 12 equal squares. Place 1 square in each muffin cup, gently pressing the puff pastry to mold into each cup. Ladle filling evenly into each of the 12 muffin cups. Top each with crumbled goat cheese.

5. Cook quiches until golden brown and egg is cooked through, about 20–25 minutes. Remove from oven and cool a bit before serving.

*Kiwifruit

Kiwis pack a significant vitamin C punch—nearly 100% of the recommended daily value in just one fruit. Some studies suggest that vitamin C is essential for healthy cognition and may influence mood and stress.

Get the facts - pg. 106

Kiwifruit Ingredient

About the blogger

Best Fruit Now - http://www.bestfruitnow.com

Tom Kovacevich
@BestFruitNow

Tom Kovacevich is in the wholesale fruit and vegetable business in Philadelphia. His company, TMK Produce, distributes top quality produce to retailers and food service companies up and down the east coast. In 2008, Tom started a blog at BestFruitNow.com as a way to share his thoughts on what fruits are best each month. Geared for consumers, BestFruitNow.com also offers tips on how to select and prepare the fruits being recommended. An avid cook, gardener, and all around foodie, Tom regularly travels the world meeting with growers to learn more about his passion: fresh produce.

Seasonal Fruit Salsa with Cinnamon Tortilla Chips

Serves 8 - 10

1 cup chopped strawberries

3 kiwifruits, peeled and chopped

¼ cup mango, chopped

½ cup pineapple, chopped

1 medium orange, peeled, seeded and chopped

¼ cup chopped red, green, or yellow bell pepper

¼ cup green onion, sliced

1 Tbsp lemon juice

1 medium jalapeño pepper, seeded and chopped

Cinnamon tortilla chips (recipe follows)

Baked Cinnamon Tortilla Chips

¼ cup sugar

½ tsp ground cinnamon

2 Tbsps melted butter

8 six inch flour tortillas

1. In a large bowl, gently combine fruits, peppers, green onions, lemon juice and jalapeño. (You can substitute other fruits as desired.)

2. Cover tightly with clear wrap, and chill for at least 1/2 hour. The salsa can be stored in the refrigerator for up to 24 hours.

Baked Cinnamon Tortilla Chips

1. Preheat oven to 350 degrees F.

2. Mix together the sugar and cinnamon and set aside.

3. Place tortillas on a cutting board, brush with butter, and thoroughly sprinkle with sugar and cinnamon.

4. Cut the tortillas into quarters and place on two cookie sheets.

5. Bake for 10–12 minutes.

6. Serve with fruit salsa.

Asparagus

What's good for the body
is often good for the brain.
Asparagus is filled with
vitamins A, C, and folic acid—
all of which may play a role
in a healthy brain just as they
do in a healthy body.

Get the facts - pg. 106

Asparagus and Fennel Salad

About the blogger

Dash and Bella - http://dashandbella.blogspot.com

Phyllis Grant
@dashandbella

Phyllis worked in pastry at New York City's Bouley, Michael's, and Nobu. She tired quickly of sugar and burning her forearms and never sleeping. Fifteen years later she started a blog called "Dash and Bella," named after her son (3) and her daughter (7). With a focus on cooking with and for children, her blog includes photos, step-by-step instructions, food preparation tips, and her own recipes for cooking delicious, seasonal, and healthful meals. She doesn't believe in "kid food," doesn't oversimplify, and involves her kids in every step of the cooking process.

Asparagus & Fennel Salad

Serves 2

1 shallot, peeled and finely diced.

1 anchovy, finely chopped, with a small amount of oil reserved

Juice and zest of ½ Meyer lemon (can substitute regular lemon)

1 tsp white wine vinegar or champagne vinegar

1 Tbsp capers with a bit of the juice

2 tsps Dijon mustard

5 Tbsps extra virgin olive oil

10 stalks of asparagus, ends trimmed, peeled up to the base of the tips, and thinly sliced on an angle

1 medium-sized head of fennel, very thinly sliced (with mandolin if possible)

3 sprigs of fennel fronds, coarsely chopped or torn

20 very thin slices of Piave cheese or Parmesan cheese (shaved with a vegetable peeler, if possible)

Coarse salt and pepper to taste

1. Place shallot and anchovy in a bowl. Add lemon juice and zest, vinegar, and capers and juice. Set aside for 10 minutes. Add mustard. Slowly whisk in olive oil and set aside.

2. Combine raw asparagus, fennel, and fennel fronds in a bowl. Add salt and pepper to taste. Toss with some of the vinaigrette and taste. Add more vinaigrette, salt, or pepper if desired, and continue tasting until salad is dressed and seasoned to your liking.

3. Sprinkle cheese over the top and gently toss once more. Serve immediately.

Sardine Ingredient

Sardine, Chickpea & Celery Salad

Serves 4

8 sardines, water or oil packed, 3¾ oz (plain or smoked, no sauce)

4 celery stalks

1 15½ oz can chickpeas, drained and rinsed

¼ cup flat leaf parsley, chopped

2 Tbsps freshly squeezed lemon juice

1 Tbsp extra virgin olive oil

½ tsp ground cumin, preferably roasted or toasted

¼ tsp kosher salt

Pinch freshly ground black pepper

1. Wash the celery and trim the tops and bottoms. Use a mandoline or a sharp knife to cut each celery stalk into very thin slices, diagonally. Combine the celery slices with the chickpeas and parsley in a serving bowl.

2. In a small bowl whisk together the lemon juice, olive oil, cumin, salt and pepper to taste. Toss the salad with the dressing and allow to sit at room temperature for 10–15 minutes to allow the flavors to meld.

3. Remove the sardines from the tin, and break each one into two pieces. Top each individual serving of salad with four sardine pieces. Serve at room temperature.

*Sardines

Sardines are great brain food because they're high in DHA— the most important fatty acid for brain health—but are low in mercury, which can harm the brain.

Get the facts - pg. 106

About the blogger

Cooking with Amy - http://cookingwithamy.blogspot.com/

Amy Sherman
@cookingwithamy

Amy Sherman created her award-winning food blog, Cooking with Amy, after friends and family continually asked her for cooking tips and restaurant recommendations. Her recipes are inspired by her experiences dining out, traveling abroad, and exploring Asian, Latino, Middle Eastern and Russian grocery stores at home. She is author of *Williams-Sonoma New Flavors for Appetizers* and *Wine Passport: Portugal*. She has also blogged about food for KQED's blog Bay Area Bites and for the Epicurious blog Epi Log, and currently blogs for Frommers.com culinary travel blog, Between Bites.

Quinoa Ingredient

Spinach & Feta Quinoa Salad

Serves 4

1 Tbsp olive oil

1 small onion, chopped finely

2 cloves garlic, chopped finely

1 bunch spinach, roughly chopped

1 cup quinoa

2 cups vegetable broth (can substitute chicken broth or water)

¼ cup parsley, chopped

¼ cup dill, chopped

¼ cup crumbled feta

Juice and zest of 1 lemon

Salt and pepper

1. Heat olive oil in a large saute pan over medium high heat. Add the onion and sauté until translucent, about 5–7 minutes.

2. Add the garlic and sauté until fragrant, about a minute. Add the spinach and cook until it wilts, about 2–4 minutes.

3. Add quinoa, broth, parsley, and dill and season with salt and pepper to taste. Bring to a boil. Reduce heat to low, cover, and simmer until the quinoa is tender, about 20 minutes.

4. Remove from heat. Add lemon juice and zest, and mix in the feta. Serve immediately.

*Quinoa

Protein-rich quinoa contains all of the essential amino acids, especially lysine, which may play a key role in regulating stress and anxiety.

Get the facts - pg. 106

About the blogger

Closet Cooking - http://closetcooking.blogspot.com

Kevin Lynch
@ClosetCooking

Kevin came to realize that his meals were boring and that he had been eating the same few dishes over and over again for years. He decided that it was time for change! Now Kevin spends all of his free time searching for and trying tasty new dishes.

Grown Up Fruit Salad Ingredients

Grown Up Fruit Salad

Serves 4

1 cup blueberries

½ cup dried cranberries

¾ cup strawberries, sliced

2 kiwifruits, peeled and thinly sliced

5 oz fresh spinach leaves

Leaves from ¾ head of romaine lettuce

¾ cup walnuts, chopped

3 oz feta or blue cheese,
   crumbled (optional)

1. Rinse all of the fruit and place in a colander lined with paper towels to dry.

2. Place the spinach and romaine in a bowl and toss together to mix.

3. Arrange berries and kiwi on top of the spinach and lettuce.

4. Top with walnuts and feta or blue cheese (if using) and serve immediately.

*Walnuts And Berries

It's hard to pick one brain food in Grown Up Fruit Salad. The berries and kiwi all have some evidence in their favor. Plus, just a quarter cup of walnuts provides nearly 100% of the recommended daily intake of omega-3 fatty acids.

Get the facts - pg. 106

About the blogger

A Southern Fairytale - http://asouthernfairytale.com

Rachel Matthews
@sthrnfairytale

Rachel Matthews is a 7th generation Texan. She's raising two rambunctious 8th Generation Texans and is wife to a wonderful Harley riding, truck driving, fishing and hunting true blue Texas gentleman. Her love of cooking developed at a young age as she stood on a chair at her Granny's side learning the glories of cast iron, butter, and southern comfort foods. While she still professes a strong love for butter and cast iron, she's constantly developing and playing with foods that are rich in the vitamins, nutrients and other things that will keep her kids' bodies and most important, their brains growing strong and staying healthy. Rachel shares her passion for food both as the Food Editor for Blissfully Domestic and on her own personal food and family blog, appropriately titled A Southern Fairytale.

*Lentils and Garbanzos

Legumes, including lentils and garbanzos, are high in folic acid. Studies suggest folic acid is good across the lifespan—from developing the baby brain to maintaining brain function in older adults.

Get the facts - pg. 106

Lentil Ingredient

About the blogger

Hangry Pants - http://www.HangryPants.com/

Heather Pare
@HangryPants

Good food has always been an important part of Heather's life. Growing up, Sundays were spent at her grandparents' house with family eating macaroni with meatballs. From making Christmas cookies with her mom, to perfecting her pancake flip with her grandpa, Heather learned about food through her family. One of Heather's favorite memories is using her grandma's hand-held mixer to prepare cake batter and licking the leftovers.

These experiences instilled an appreciation for family and food traditions. When cooking for herself and her family, Heather tries to recreate these memories in her own life.

Lentil & Squash Salad

Serves 4

1 medium zucchini, sliced into ½ inch thick circles

1 medium summer squash, sliced into ½ inch thick circles

7 Tbsps extra virgin olive oil, divided

1 tsp garlic powder (or more, to taste)

1 tsp Romano cheese, grated (or more, to taste)

1 cup cooked lentils

1 15½ oz can of garbanzo beans, rinsed and drained

5 sprigs fresh dill, chopped

¼ cup red onion, chopped

2 tsp balsamic vinegar

Salt and pepper, to taste

1. Preheat the oven to 425 degrees F.

2. Place zucchini and squash circles on a baking sheet and drizzle with 2 tablespoons extra virgin olive oil, garlic powder, and Romano cheese. Roast in the oven until crispy and lightly browned, about 20 minutes. Remove from oven and set aside.

3. Place lentils, garbanzo beans, dill, and onion in a large bowl. Pour the remaining olive oil from the baking sheet into the bowl, and add the squash and zucchini.

4. In a small bowl, whisk together balsamic vinegar, remaining 5 tablespoons olive oil, and salt and pepper to taste. Pour over salad and toss to combine.

5. Sprinkle on more Romano cheese (if desired) and serve immediately.

*Spinach

Spinach and its leafy green relatives are true superfoods, packing in almost 400% of the recommended daily value of vitamin A in just 1 cup—which is good for your brain and your body.

Get the facts - pg. 106

Spinach Ingredient

About the blogger

My Cooking Hut - http://www.mycookinghut.com

Leemei Tan

Leemei has always been passionate about food. She comes from Malaysia, the country where culinary diversity is found through its multicultural populations of Malay, Indian, Eurasian, Chinese, Nyonya and the indigenous people of Borneo.

Her upbringing in a multiethnic society has great influence in her cooking. She is neither a trained chef nor a home economist. Her style of cooking has always been practical, simple, healthy and delicious. Her travel experiences have also greatly inspired her in creating new recipes. She cooks Asian, Modern French and Franco-Asian dishes.

Spinach Salad Campagnarde-Style

Serves 2

2 cups baby spinach

½ cup cherry tomatoes, cut in half

3 strips lardons (or bacon), diced

2 eggs

2 medium potatoes, peeled and diced

A handful of croutons

Dressing:

4 Tbsps extra virgin olive oil

1 Tbsp balsamic vinegar

½ tsp Dijon mustard

Salt and pepper

1. To make the dressing, whisk olive oil, balsamic vinegar, Dijon mustard, and salt and pepper to taste. Set aside.

2. Pan fry the lardons (or bacon) until they are golden brown and crispy. Dice and set aside.

3. Boil the potatoes in a pot of salted water until tender, about 15-20 minutes. Set aside to let them cool.

4. Place eggs in a pot of cold water. Bring to a boil over medium heat, then reduce heat and simmer 12 minutes. Turn off heat and let cool. Remove the shells, then quarter the boiled eggs.

5. To make the salad, combine baby spinach, cherry tomatoes, and potatoes in a salad bowl and toss to mix well. Split between 2 plates. Sprinkle half of the lardons (or bacon) on each salad. Add croutons. Arrange egg quarters on top of the salad. Drizzle dressing over the salad and serve immediately.

Curried Wheat Berry & Tomato Salad

Curried Wheat Berry & Tomato Salad

Serves 6

1 cup wheat berries

5 Tbsps extra virgin olive oil

3 Tbsps fresh lemon juice

2 tsps curry powder

1 cup tomatoes, chopped

1 spring onion, sliced

1 Tbsp fresh parsley, chopped

Salt and pepper to taste

1. Place the wheat berries in a large saucepan and add 3 1/2 cups water. Bring to a boil, then cover, reduce heat, and simmer until tender, about 45 minutes to one hour. Drain and rinse with cool water. Set aside.

2. Meanwhile, make the dressing. In a bowl, whisk together olive oil, lemon juice, curry powder, and salt and pepper to taste. Set aside.

3. In a serving bowl, toss together wheat berries, tomatoes, onion, and parsley.

4. Pour dressing over salad, toss to coat, and serve immediately.

*Tomatoes

High amounts of lycopene aren't found in many foods, but tomatoes are a great source. That means tomatoes may have unique brain-healthy properties: lycopene has been associated with better brain function.

Get the facts - pg. 106

About the blogger

Fake Food Free - http://www.fakefoodfree.com

Lori Rice
@lori1329

Lori's interests in food and health motivated her to earn a Master's degree in nutrition. Through travel and living abroad she has had the opportunity to explore foods of different cultures and her passion for food has grown because of these experiences. She believes that real, quality food should be savored and enjoyed. The foods we have eaten throughout history should be respected, as well as those who know the traditional ways of preparing them. Lori strives to be sustainable, more local, beyond organic and respectful in her food choices while embracing the cultures and foods from all around this world. Her blog serves as a creative outlet to share her passion for cooking, real food, travel and wellness.

Olive Oil Ingredient

Goat Cheese Toasts With Arugula

Serves 4

⅓ cup fresh basil leaves, finely chopped

½ cup of olive oil, divided

4 thick slices of crusty bread

1 garlic clove, cut lengthwise in half

6 oz of goat cheese cut into ¾ inch slices

5 cups of arugula

Juice from one small lemon

Salt and freshly cracked black pepper

Pitted olives (optional)

1. In a mortar and pestle, mash the basil together with 1/4 cup olive oil to make a watery paste. Set aside for at least 1 hour.

2. Preheat the oven to 450 degrees F.

3. Rub each slice of bread with the cut side of the garlic clove and place the bread on a baking pan. Top with goat cheese slices and bake for roughly 8–10 minutes, or until toasted. Remove from oven and top each piece with the basil sauce.

4. Whisk together the lemon juice, remaining 1/4 cup olive oil and salt and pepper to taste. Toss the arugula with the dressing.

5. To serve, place arugula on a plate and top with the goat cheese toasts and basil sauce.

6. Scatter pitted olives on the plate if desired.

*Olive Oil

Studies suggest a Mediterranean diet rich in olive oil is good for the brain. That may be because fish, olives, legumes, and other staples of the diet all contain brain-healthy nutrients. Olive oil is rich in polyphenols—a group of chemicals that may protect against Alzheimer's.

Get the facts - pg. 106

About the blogger

Lisa's Kitchen - http://foodandspice.blogspot.com

Lisa Turner

Based in London, Ontario, Canada, Lisa is a veteran vegetarian of 19 years, serving up a collection of delicious culinary creations from her kitchen. Inspired by cuisines from around the world, Lisa emphasizes healthy vegetarian food and spicy Indian dishes. If you want to know what sensible vegetarians eat, Lisa's Kitchen is the place to be.

Spinach Dhal - Photo Courtesy of Cynthia Nelson

Spinach Dhal

Serves 4

1 cup yellow split peas or split moong dal, soaked overnight in water

1 whole hot pepper of your choice

3 cups fresh spinach leaves, washed and dried

2 Tbsps vegetable or canola oil

1 tsp black mustard seeds (can substitute yellow or brown mustard seeds)

1 tsp cumin seeds

2 large cloves garlic, thinly sliced

Salt to taste

1. Rinse soaked peas twice, drain, and add to a 4 or 5 quart pot. Add 5 cups water and the whole hot pepper and stir.

2. Cover pot, place over high heat, and bring to a boil. Let peas cook until you have the consistency of a pea soup. Most of the peas should have melted; use the back of your spoon to mash.

3. Once the desired consistency has been reached, add the spinach and season the peas with salt to taste. Cover and reduce heat to low.

4. While the peas are simmering, heat oil in a small frying pan over medium heat. Toss in mustard seeds. When the mustard seeds begin to pop, add the cumin and cook for 30 seconds more. Add the garlic and cook until it just starts to color.

5. Remove spice mixture from heat and pour the contents into the simmering dhal. Stir everything together and let it simmer for one minute more.

6. Remove from heat and serve with rice, roti, or bread—or eat it as a soup.

*Split Peas

Split peas and other legumes are rich in folic acid, which in research studies has been shown to improve verbal and memory performance, and may delay the onset of Alzheimer's disease.

Get the facts - pg. 106

About the blogger

Tastes Like Home - http://www.tasteslikehome.org

Cynthia Nelson

Cynthia Nelson has been a media professional for more than 17 years. She has travelled extensively through the Caribbean, savoring and learning the cuisine of the region. Born in Guyana, she is currently based in Barbados and is a tutor of Mass Communication. Cynthia's musings on food and life appear regularly in publications in the Caribbean and North America. She is the author of the cookbook *Tastes Like Home* by Ian Randle Publishers, due out in October, 2010, and the award-winning blog, Tastes Like Home.

Turmeric

If you're looking for brain health, make sure your curry powder contains turmeric. Even a small amount of curcumin—a compound in turmeric—can be beneficial to the brain. It's one of the reasons scientists believe India has much lower levels of dementia.

Get the facts - pg. 106

Curry Powder Ingredient

About the blogger

Gourmet Fury - http://www.GourmetFury.com

Melody Fury
@GourmetFury

Melody Fury is Vancouver's modern food culture and lifestyle ambassador. The VancouverFoodTour.com entrepreneur showcases her city through her diverse culinary insight, engaging personality, and dynamic presentation styles. She is a food and travel writer by day, wine and cocktail ninja by night. With a spare moment, she cooks up a storm and documents her recipes and photos in her blog. GourmetFury.com is nominated for Best Canadian Blog (10th Annual Weblog Awards), Best Food Blog, and Best Travel Blog (2010 Canadian Weblog Awards). In the same year, Melody also received four Foodbuzz Award nominations.

Curry Grilled Corn Soup

Serves 4

3 ears of corn, shucked
 and cleaned

½ yellow onion, diced

½ head garlic, minced

2 Tbsps yellow curry powder

2 sweet bell peppers, diced

8 cups chicken or vegetable stock

½ cup fresh basil, chiffonade
 (rolled up and sliced into
 thin strips)

Zest and juice of 1 lime

Freshly minced chili to taste

1 tsp brown sugar

Salt and pepper to taste

Olive oil for grilling and sautéing

1. Rub corn with olive oil and salt to taste. Heat a charcoal or flame grill. Using tongs, grill the corn until blistered and brown. Set aside to cool, then hold corn upright over a plate and carefully sliced the kernels off the cob with a knife.

2. Meanwhile, sweat the onions in a pot with a bit of olive oil until translucent. Add the garlic and curry powder and cook until fragrant. Add the bell peppers and sweat for another 2 minutes.

3. Add grilled corn and chicken or vegetable stock to the pot. Bring to a boil, lower to medium heat, and simmer for 5 minutes to incorporate the flavors. Adjust with more water if desired.

4. Remove the soup from the heat. Add the basil, chili, lime zest and juice, and brown sugar.

5. Taste and adjust seasoning if desired. Serve hot, garnished with thinly sliced pepper and basil.

*Kale

If it's leafy and dark green, it's full of brain-boosting antioxidants. Kale is no exception to that rule!

Get the facts - pg. 106

Napa Farmhouse 1885 Beans & Greens

About the blogger

Napa Farmhouse 1885 - http://www.napafarmhouse1885.blogspot.com

Diane Padoven
@napafarmhouse

Diane's lifelong love of terrific-tasting ingredients started when she would spend a few weeks at her grandparents' home during summer vacations. She and her grandmother would visit a small open-air produce stand daily to buy fresh ingredients. From those experiences, Diane developed a belief that using quality ingredients is an investment in your health, leads to the best tasting food, supports small farmers, and helps green the earth.

When she purchased a farmhouse in the Napa Valley of California, Diane began to preserve foods, create her own seasoning blends, and grow herbs, fruit, and veggies organically. When Diane used to go on business trips to Europe, her associates would go crazy buying shoes, handbags and clothes, and she was the one lugging back tins of extra virgin olive oil, vinegars, and seasonings.

Napa Farmhouse 1885
Beans & Greens

Serves 6-8

4 cups dried pinto beans

2 Tbsps extra virgin olive oil

1 onion, chopped

3 cloves garlic, minced

1 large carrot, chopped

2½ cups kale leaves, stem and center rib removed, chopped (note: any type of kale can be used)

1 cup tomato sauce

3 Tbsps chili powder (or to taste)

1 Tbsp dried oregano

1 tsp cinnamon

1 tsp dark chocolate cocoa powder

1 canned chipotle pepper in adobo sauce, minced, with 1 tsp-1 Tbsp adobo sauce reserved

Sea salt

Freshly cracked black pepper

1. Rinse beans and place in large pot and cover with 8 cups water. Allow to soak overnight.

2. The next day, heat olive oil in a pan and sauté onion, garlic, carrot and kale until onions are translucent. Add to bean pot.

3. Add tomato sauce, chili powder, oregano, cinnamon, cocoa powder, chipotle, and adobo sauce to pot. Bring to a boil, stirring occasionally. When boiling, reduce heat to a simmer, cover and cook for approximately one hour. Add extra water if necessary.

4. Beans are ready when they mash easily when pressed with the back of a spoon. Remove from heat and add salt and pepper to taste.

5. Beans can be kept in refrigerator for a few days, or frozen for up to three months.

Eggs Baked in Cream

Eggs Baked in Cream

Serves 1

1 Tbsp butter

¼ cup leeks, sliced, (white and light green parts only)

2 sprigs parsley leaves, roughly chopped

1-2 tsps harissa

1 large egg

2 Tbsps half-and-half

Salt and coarsely ground black pepper

Rustic bread, toasted

1. Set an oven rack in the middle of the oven and preheat oven to 400 degrees F.

2. Melt butter over medium heat in a small sauté pan and add sliced leeks with a splash of water and a pinch or two of salt. Cook until leeks are tender, soft, and caramelized, about 20 minutes.

3. Transfer leeks to a ramekin or a small baking dish and line the bottom of the dish with them. Sprinkle parsley leaves on top, reserving a few bits for garnish. Spread the harissa over the herbs in a thin layer, using as much as desired.

4. Crack the egg and gently slide it into the middle of the dish. Add the cream so it covers the egg white. Sprinkle with salt and pepper to taste.

5. Bake egg for 8–12 minutes, until cooked to your liking. Serve immediately with grilled or toasted bread.

*Eggs

Not surprisingly, eggs have something in common with chicken: high choline content. Choline is associated with long-term memory development.

Get the facts - pg. 106

About the blogger

Sassy Radish - http://www.sassyradish.com

Olga Massov
@sassyradish

Sassy Radish is a blog written by Olga Massov, a finance geek by day and home cook enthusiast by night. Sassy Radish is dedicated to cooking, writing and photography. Initially the blog was conceived with the notion that good food need not be complicated, and that cooking with whole ingredients was not only a way of cooking, it was a reflection on how we live our lives. Also, cooking is simply fun.

Originally, Olga hails from Russia, and although she's lived in the United States most her life, she maintains her deep love of all things pickled, herring, pelmeni, cabbage, and sour cream (among other things). Olga's life in the US, on the other hand, helped her to develop great penchant for things like bourbon, barbecue, and bluegrass. She likes to eat pretty much everything, particularly sushi, brisket, Indian, Thai, and good Mexican (the latter being rather difficult to locate in New York). She's a sucker for things with cilantro, lime, and onions, and thinks mashed potatoes is an acceptable answer to a really bad day.

***Spinach**

Aside from the doses of vitamins A, C, and E, spinach is also a great source of folic acid—something your brain needs for healthy functioning from conception to old age.

Get the facts - pg. 106

Spinach & Caramelized Onion Tart

About the blogger

Shelterrific - http://www.shelterrific.com

Erica Policow

Erica was one of those kids who only ate PB&J with the crust cut off, grilled cheese sandwiches with Kraft Singles and chicken nuggets. The only green food she'd let past her lips had a chocolate center and a hard candy shell. So how did the world's pickiest eater become a food editor with only one known dislike on her list (cilantro)? She moved to New York City, that's how. With everything she could possibly want to eat at her fingertips, she was suddenly tempted to try it all. These days, she is lucky to be able to share her passion with others through blogging, cooking and recipe development.

Spinach & Caramelized Onion Tart

Serves 6

Crust

1¼ cups flour

½ cup cold water

¾ cup cornmeal, preferably stone ground

1 tsp fine-grain sea salt

¼ cup olive oil

Filling

1 Tbsp olive oil

1 large yellow onion, halved then thinly sliced

2 cloves garlic, minced

1 tsp fresh thyme leaves

12 oz baby spinach leaves (can substitute regular spinach leaves, roughly chopped)

6 oz cream cheese

2 eggs

⅓ cup milk, preferably 2%

Crust

1. In a medium bowl, whisk together the flour, cornmeal, and salt. Slowly add the oil in a thin stream while stirring constantly with a fork. Slowly add 1/2 cup cold water in a thin stream, stirring constantly with a fork, mixing until absorbed.

2. With your hand, work the dough until it just comes together into a ball inside of the bowl. Turn dough out onto a surface dusted with cornmeal and roll into an 11- to 12-inch circle. Lightly oil a 9- or 10-inch tart pan and line the pan with the dough circle. Gently press into pan and remove excess dough from around the edges. Set the tart shell on a baking sheet and refrigerate while you prepare the filling.

Filling

1. In a large skillet, heat the olive oil over medium heat. Add the onion and cook, stirring occasionally, until caramelized, about 20–25 minutes.

2. Add garlic and thyme and cook 1 minute more, stirring constantly. Turn the heat up to medium-high and add 1/3 of the spinach leaves. Toss the spinach around in the pan, mixing it with the onions, until it begins to wilt. Mix in the remaining spinach in 2 batches, until it is wilted and incorporated with the onions. Remove from heat and season to taste with salt and pepper.

3. Preheat the oven to 400 degrees F. In a blender or food processor, combine the cream cheese, eggs, and milk and pulse until well mixed.

4. Spread the onion-spinach mixture over the bottom of the prepared tart shell, then top with the cream cheese mixture. Bake for 35–40 minutes, or until the egg is set and the top is a light golden brown. Remove from oven and let sit 10 minutes before slicing.

Eggs

Eggs are rich in choline, a key ingredient in the neurotransmitter acetylcholine (ACh). Acetylcholine is necessary for healthy communication between brain cells.

Get the facts - pg. 106

Egg Ingredient

About the blogger

The Leftover Queen - http://www.leftoverqueen.com/

Jenn Campus
@leftoverqueen

Jenn is a homespun cook who blogs about using leftovers and pantry essentials to make frugal, healthy and delicious meals, using local, seasonal and traditional foods. She gives her readers tips on how to easily incorporate this philosophy into busy lifestyles, advocating healthy eating for the young, old, economically challenged and everyone in between.

Jenn loves to discuss fitness as it relates to food. She enjoys activities like archery, weight lifting and hiking. This has led to a passion for creating nourishing foods full of the nutrients needed to give her the energy to do what she loves.

Jenn's "Breakfast of Champions"

Serves 2

1 Tbsp olive oil

½ cup cooked buckwheat (kasha)

1 cup chard, cleaned and
roughly chopped

1 tsp Herbs de Provence
(can substitute your favorite
dried green herb, like thyme,
tarragon, or dill)

¼ cup goat cheese, crumbled

2 eggs

Salt and pepper

1. In a large skillet (preferably cast iron), over medium heat, sauté the buckwheat in the olive oil for 2-3 minutes, until browned.

2. Add the greens to the skillet and sauté with the buckwheat, until greens are wilted.

3. Season with Herbs de Provence (or whichever herb you're using.) Crumble the goat cheese on top.

4. Create two piles of the sautéed mixture, on opposite sides of the pan. Crack the eggs on top of each pile of the sauté and season the eggs with salt and pepper to taste.

5. Lower the heat to lowest setting, place a lid on the skillet, and cook until eggs are cooked to your liking. Remove each serving to a plate and serve immediately.

*Asparagus

Asparagus is full of vitamin A, which contributes to adult brain plasticity—helping you keep your brain learning and growing as you age.

Get the facts - pg. 106

Asparagus, Mushroom and Ham Quiche with a Potato Crust

About the blogger

For the Love of Cooking - http://fortheloveofcooking-recipes.blogspot.com

Pam Nelson

Pam is a stay-at-home mom with two children who inspire her to be a better cook. She loves using fresh ingredients, organic when possible, and likes to experiment with different tastes and textures. She tries to keep her recipes lower in fat but still tasting great. Her favorite hobbies are cooking, photography and blogging so she decided to combine them and create a recipe blog. It has been a wonderful way for her to organize her recipes and share them at the same time.

Asparagus, Mushroom & Ham Quiche with a Potato Crust

Serves 6

1-2 russet potatoes, sliced very thinly

1 tsp olive oil

½ sweet yellow onion, diced

4 oz button mushrooms, sliced

8 grape tomatoes, cut in half

1 cup ham, diced

5 asparagus spears, ends removed, cut into thirds

¼ cup Swiss cheese, shredded (more if desired)

8 eggs, beaten

¼ cup of milk

Sea salt and freshly cracked pepper

Cooking spray

1. Preheat the oven to 375 degrees F.

2. Coat a pie pan with cooking spray. Layer thin slices of potato in the pan, overlapping, to completely cover the bottom and sides. Spray with cooking spray again and bake in the oven for 7–10 minutes. Remove from oven and set aside.

3. Meanwhile, heat the olive oil in a large skillet over medium heat. Add the onions and mushrooms and season to taste with salt. Sauté the onions and mushrooms for 5–7 minutes or until golden brown and tender.

4. Distribute onions, mushrooms, asparagus, tomatoes, diced ham, and Swiss cheese in the potato crust.

5. Beat eggs and milk together, and season with salt and pepper to taste. Pour the egg mixture on top of the veggies and ham.

6. Place quiche in the oven and bake for 30–40 minutes, or until a knife inserted in the center of the quiche comes out clean.

7. Remove from oven and let cool for a few minutes before slicing.

*Onion

Onions are rich in the antioxidant quercetin, which has been shown to protect against stroke and may improve impaired memory.

Get the facts - pg. 106

Onion Ingredient

About the blogger

Off The Broiler - http://offthebroiler.com

Jason Perlow
@jperlow

Jason Perlow is widely considered to be one of the founders of modern food blogging, with his launching of the eGullet.com food discussion site in 2001. In 2006 he founded the critically acclaimed food blog Off The Broiler, which quickly gained a healthier cooking and eating focus after he decided to make some important life changes. Jason enjoys outdoor grilling and traditional Southern barbecue, Asian and other multicultural cuisines, and is an avid proponent of integrating vegetarian meals into a well balanced diet.

Spicy Portobello Chili

Serves 4-6

1 tsp olive oil

1 cup yellow onion, diced

5 cups Portobello mushroom caps, chopped (about 4-5 mushroom caps)

4 cloves garlic, minced

1 14½ oz can diced tomatoes with chili

1 can beans (pinto, black, or red kidney)

½ cup textured vegetable protein

2 tsp ground cumin

2 Tbsps high quality ground chili powder such as chipotle or guajillo

1 tsp salt

Large handful pomegranate seeds

½ cup red or green onion, diced

½ cup shredded cheddar cheese or vegan cheese substitute (optional)

Chopped cilantro to taste (optional)

1. Heat olive oil in a large pot over medium-high heat. Add yellow onions and sauté until browned.

2. Add mushrooms, garlic, canned tomatoes, beans, textured vegetable protein, cumin, chili powder, salt, and 3 cups of water. Bring to a boil, simmer and cook for about 20–25 minutes (or to desired thickness).

3. Serve in a bowl or over brown rice or a baked potato. Garnish with red or green onion and pomegranate seeds (and cheese and cilantro, if using).

Browned Butter & Sage Gnocchi

Browned Butter & Sage Gnocchi

Serves 2

2 servings gnocchi

3 Tbsps salted butter

10 fresh sage leaves

½ tsp lemon juice

Sea salt and ground black pepper

Grated Parmesan cheese (optional)

1. Fill a large saucepan with water, add a pinch of salt and bring to a boil.

2. Add gnocchi to boiling water and cook for 2 minutes or until they float to the surface. Remove with a slotted spoon or drain in a colander and set aside.

3. Place a large frying pan over medium heat. Add butter to the hot pan and let it gently melt and brown.

4. Turn up the heat and add sage leaves. Sage leaves will begin to fry, curling and crisping up.

5. Remove the sage leaves.

6. Add cooked gnocchi to hot butter in pan. Toss quickly to evenly sear the gnocchi.

7. Season with salt, pepper and lemon juice, tossing as you go.

8. Return fried sage leaves to gnocchi and serve immediately with some freshly grated Parmesan cheese.

*Sage

Sage has long been thought to have medicinal properties, and current science has borne that out. Sage has been shown to help your memory and may improve outcomes for those with Alzheimer's disease.

Get the facts - pg. 106

About the blogger

The Sugar Bar - http://www.sugarbar.org

Davina Lim
@sugarbardiva

She shops, she eats, she writes. The smell of baking muffins is her eau de parfum and the sizzling of hot fat in a pan, music to her ears! A baking obsession that began in high school has now exploded into a Madhatter-style approach to all things related to cooking and dessert. It's chaotic and experimental in the kitchen because she is an open-minded foodie, eager to taste what the world can offer. But Mama's cooking is truly the best.

So she never forgets the classic, the unpretentious and the homely or the fact that the humblest of kitchens and ingredients can still capture the hearts of many.

*Garbanzo beans

Garbanzo beans and other legumes are rich in folic acid—great for the developing brain. Pregnant women should make sure to get an adequate supply of folic acid to ensure good brain health for their babies.

Get the facts - pg. 106

Chana Masala with Mushrooms - Photo Courtesy of Michael Natkin

About the blogger

Herbivoracious - http://herbivoracious.com

Michael Natkin
@michaelnatkin

Michael a software engineer by day and an aspiring chef by night. He has been a vegetarian for over 25 years, and is always learning about new techniques and ingredients. He has staged at some of Seattle's best restaurants and hopes to start a full time culinary career soon. In the meantime, Herbivoracious.com has become an incredible way for him to connect with other cooks and share his passion for vibrant, full flavored vegetarian food.

Chana Masala with Mushrooms

Serves 2-4

1 15-oz can chickpeas, drained and rinsed, or 1½ cups home-cooked chickpeas

3 Tbsps vegetable oil or clarified butter, divided

1 Tbsp black mustard seeds, divided

1 tsp fennel seeds

1 tsp cumin seeds

1 tsp coriander seeds

2 cloves garlic, minced

½ medium onion, diced finely

1 medium tomato, cored, diced finely (can substitute canned diced tomatoes)

1⅓ cups white mushrooms, quartered or thickly sliced

1 small, hot red chili pepper, thinly sliced (add gradually)

1 Tbsp fresh grated turmeric (can substitute 2 tsps dry turmeric)

¼ tsp cinnamon

1 pinch ground cloves

¼ tsp cayenne pepper

2 Tbsps lemon juice

1 tsp salt

Cilantro for garnish

1. Drain and rinse chickpeas. Place them in a saucepan with water to cover, then bring to a boil and simmer until soft. (You can skip this step if your chickpeas are already soft.)

2. In a large skillet, heat 2 tablespoons oil or clarified butter over a medium-high flame. Add 2 teaspoons mustard seed, fennel, cumin, and coriander seeds. Cook for about 10–20 seconds until the mustard seeds begin to pop. Immediately add the garlic, onion, and tomato.

3. Cook, stirring occasionally, for about 5 minutes until the liquid is mostly gone and everything is browning.

4. Drain the chickpeas and add them, with mushrooms, a small amount of the hot pepper, turmeric, cinnamon, cloves, cayenne pepper, lemon juice, 1 teaspoon of salt, and a cup of water. It will be soupy.

5. Cook uncovered over a medium-low flame for about 15 minutes, until the sauce begins to thicken. Does it need more salt? More lemon juice? A bit more cayenne? Finish for the texture you want.

6. In a separate skillet, heat the remaining tablespoon of oil over a high flame and fry remaining 1 teaspoon mustard seeds until they pop. (This is called tempering, and it is a great way to add a final layer of flavor.) Toss the contents of that skillet over the chickpeas, garnish with cilantro, and serve.

* Chili peppers can be extremely hot with the seeds containing most of the heat. It is a good idea to remove the seeds, mince the pepper and gradually add it in (until you achieve the heat you prefer) and add the seeds if necessary. It is important to always wash your hands after handling a hot pepper, because the heat can remain on your hands and transfer to your eyes, face, etc.

*Shrimp

Shrimp has some of those brain-boosting DHAs, but also offers a dose of vitamin B12, which has been demonstrated to be one of the most important vitamins for cognitive health and neuroprotection.

Get the facts - pg. 106

Orecchiette with Spinach, Shrimp and Garlic Chips

About the blogger

Chocolate Shavings - http://www.chocolateshavings.ca

Jennifer Bartoli
@ChocShavings

Jennifer Bartoli grew up in Paris, France and has been cooking for as long as she could hold a spoon. After graduating from McGill University, she decided to follow her longstanding passion for food and moved to New York City to study at the French Culinary Institute. She is now living and working in Montreal as a food photographer, journalist and recipe developer and can most often be found browsing piles of cookbooks while thinking of what dish to try in the kitchen next.

Orecchiette with Spinach, Shrimp and Garlic Chips

Serves 2

½ lb orecchiette
  (or your favorite small pasta)

12 uncooked shrimp, peeled
  and deveined

4 large garlic cloves, peeled
  and cut into thin slices

2 cups baby spinach leaves

Juice and zest of ½ a lemon

3 Tbsps freshly grated
  Parmesan cheese

Extra virgin olive oil for sautéing

Salt and freshly ground pepper

1. Cook pasta according to package instructions.

2. Meanwhile, put a good drizzle of olive oil in a pan on medium low heat. Add the garlic slices. Cook until the garlic flavors the oil and turns a light shade of golden brown, about 4–5 minutes. Remove garlic from pan with a slotted spoon and reserve.

3. Add the shrimp to the pan and season to taste with salt and pepper. Increase heat to medium. As soon as the shrimp turns opaque and pink in color, add the spinach leaves and drizzle with a little more olive oil. Season again with salt and pepper.

4. Once the pasta is cooked, drain it and add it to the pan with about a teaspoon of the pasta water and gently stir everything together. Add the lemon juice and zest, garlic chips, and Parmesan cheese. Drizzle with a little extra virgin olive oil and serve immediately.

*Almonds

Nuts are infamously high in calories—but also high in nutrients. The vitamin E in almonds may decrease the risk of coronary artery disease and slow Alzheimer's.

Get the facts - pg. 106

Spicy Almond Soba Noodles

About the blogger

The Way the Cookie Crumbles - http://www.o-cookies.blogspot.com

Erin O'Leary Stewart
@erinocookies

A dancer and a foodie living in the heart of the West Village in New York, Erin worked for top restaurateurs upon moving to the city while focusing on a career in dance. Her love for delectable dishes and her passion for fitness and health intersected with the founding of O'Cookies Wholesome Bites, her original line of healthy cookies made with all natural and organic ingredients with some vegan options. Erin is a Physique 57 instructor and writes the blog The Way the Cookie Crumbles about all things food, flavor and fitness.

Spicy Almond Soba Noodles

Serves 2

4 oz buckwheat soba noodles

1 garlic clove, minced

2 tsp fresh ginger, minced

2 scallions, cut into thin slices

½ red bell pepper, seeded, thinly sliced then chopped

½ cup shredded cabbage

½ cup blanched broccoli florets or broccolini, chopped into bite-size pieces

¼ cup almond slivers, toasted

Extra-virgin olive oil

Spicy almond sauce (recipe follows)

Spicy Almond Sauce

½ cup raw almond butter (recipe follows)

¼ cup rice vinegar

2 tsps agave nectar

1 tsp ginger, peeled and chopped

2-3 Tbsps crushed red chili flakes, depending on how spicy you like it

Sea salt, to taste

Raw Almond Butter

2 cups shelled almonds

3 Tbsps almond oil or coconut oil

Pinch of salt (optional)

Raw Almond Butter

1. Place almonds in a food processor or high-speed blender and process until they become fine crumbs. Add in salt (if using) and oil a bit at a time and process more until it becomes a smooth paste, adding more oil to reach desired texture. Transfer in a jar and keep refrigerated. Makes a 10-oz jar.

Spicy Almond Sauce

1. Blend the almond butter, rice vinegar, agave, ginger, and crushed red pepper flakes to taste in a food processor or high-speed blender until completely smooth. Add hot water as needed to reach the desired consistency (about 3 teaspoons.) Add salt to taste and adjust seasoning if necessary. This can be made in advance and kept in the refrigerator for up to a week.

To Cook and Serve

1. Bring a large pot of water to a boil and add a pinch of salt and a splash of olive oil. Add the soba noodles and cook until just tender, about 10 minutes. Drain and set aside.

2. In a large sauté pan or wok, heat a splash of olive oil over high heat. Add the garlic, ginger, cabbage, and broccoli and sauté for 5–10 minutes until desired crispness.

3. Remove vegetables from heat, add the noodles, and toss with the dressing, scallions and red bell pepper. Top with toasted almond slivers and additional spicy almond sauce, if desired.

Tuna

In addition to brain-boosting, omega-3 fatty acids, tuna also has a significant amount of niacin—which has been identified as one of the most important nutrients for optimal cognition and neuroprotection.

Get the facts - pg. 106

Tuna Ingredient

About the blogger

Seriously Good - http://seriouslygood.kdweeks.com

Kevin D. Weeks
@KDWeeks

At various times Kevin has earned a living as a bluegrass musician, store manager, baker, computer programmer, magazine editor, waiter, and a few other things. Although this list implies a short attention span, during all those years—in fact, since he was six years old—he has been a cook. As a cook he sought food that gave him pause, dishes that demanded his attention, and flavors that evoked passion. Kevin seeks food that is seriously good. He currently lives in Knoxville, Tennessee, and perhaps inevitably, he is a personal chef, cooking instructor, and food writer.

Baked Tuna and Rotini

Serves 4

¾ cup vegetable stock

½ cup dry vermouth, divided

Juice of 2 lemons

1 8 to 12 oz tuna steak

½ lb rotini or fusilli

4 Tbsps olive oil, divided

¼ cup onion, diced

¼ cup bell pepper, diced (green or ripe)

2 cloves garlic, chopped

1 cup cherry tomatoes, halved

Leaves from 2 sprigs fresh oregano,
  coarsely chopped

Pinch of red pepper flakes

⅔ cup low-fat mozzarella, shredded

3 Tbsps Parmigiano, shredded

Salt and pepper to taste

1. Combine vegetable stock, 1/4 cup vermouth, and lemon juice in a 10-inch, lidded skillet and bring to a boil.

2. Reduce heat to low, add steak, cover, and cook for 10 minutes, turning tuna halfway through. Remove from heat, break tuna into flakes with a fork, and set it aside.

3. Cook rotini according to package directions, drain, and set aside.

4. Preheat oven to 425 degrees F.

5. Heat 2 tablespoons of olive oil in a skillet over medium heat. Sauté onions and bell pepper until onions are translucent. Add garlic and cook one minute longer. Add remaining 1/4 cup vermouth and reduce to about one tablespoon. Add tomatoes, oregano, and red pepper and cook two minutes longer.

6. Combine tuna, vegetable mixture, cheeses, rotini, salt and pepper and remaining 2 tablespoons of olive oil in a large bowl.

7. Scoop into a casserole dish, cover tightly with foil, and bake 30 minutes.

Onions, garbanzos, garlic, spinach

This dish offers a powerhouse of brain benefits—combining antioxidant-rich spinach, brain-boosting alliums like onions and garlic, folic acid from the garbanzo beans, and much more.

Get the facts - pg. 106

Chicken & Pecan Enchiladas

About the blogger

Project Foodie - http://www.projectfoodie.com

Pam Thuman-Commike
@projectfoodie

Pam is the Chief Foodie at Project Foodie. She is a lifelong foodie who loves to cook, try new recipes and enjoy great food. After spending a day searching stacks of magazines for a particular recipe she wanted to serve at a party, Pam knew there had to be a better way. The result is Project Foodie: a one-stop recipe search website with over 100,000 recipes that lets foodies everywhere easily find their favorite magazine, newspaper, TV, and cookbook recipes without needing to remember when or where they were published.

Chicken & Pecan Enchiladas

Serves 6

4 poblano peppers

2 bunches spinach, washed and trimmed (about 12 cups)

2 onions, sliced (about 2 cups), divided

4 cloves garlic, minced, divided

1 15½ oz can garbanzo beans, with liquid

2 Tbsps pecans

½ cup chicken broth

1¼ tsps cumin, divided

1 Tbsp fresh lemon juice

1 lb boneless skinless chicken breasts

1 lb cremini mushrooms, trimmed and sliced

1 red bell pepper, cut in strips

2 Tbsps chopped cilantro, plus extra for garnish

6 10" flour tortillas

1½ cup shredded mozzarella (optional)

Salt and pepper to taste

Vegetable oil for sautéing

1. Char whole poblano peppers under broiler until skin is blackened. Remove from broiler and put in sealed plastic zip bag. Let sit for 15 minutes, then peel, seed and cut peppers into 1/2-inch strips. Set aside.

2. Boil water in a large pot. Add spinach and blanch for 30–60 seconds in boiling water. Drain and rinse with cold water. Let cool. Squeeze out excess water and set aside.

3. Heat a bit of oil in a pan and sauté 1 cup of onions until golden, 5–10 minutes. Add half of the minced garlic and cook 1 more minute.

4. Add half of the poblano pepper strips and all of the spinach. Sauté for 1 or 2 minutes to combine. Remove from heat and set aside.

5. Place garbanzo beans and liquid in a blender. Add pecans, poblano-onion-spinach mixture, chicken broth, 1/4 tsp cumin, lemon juice, and salt and pepper to taste. Blend until smooth. Set sauce aside.

6. Preheat oven to 350 degrees F. While oven is heating, grill chicken breasts approximately 4 minutes per side until cooked through. Remove from grill, shred chicken with a fork, and set aside.

7. While chicken is grilling, sauté remaining cup of onions in a bit of oil until soft, about 5 minutes. Add remaining half of the minced garlic and cook 1 minute. Add mushrooms and sauté until the liquid evaporates. Remove from heat.

8. Add remaining poblano pepper strips, red bell pepper strips, shredded chicken breast, remaining teaspoon of cumin, and chopped cilantro to onion-mushroom mixture and stir to combine. Season to taste with salt and pepper.

9. Working one tortilla at a time, heat a tortilla in the microwave for 15 seconds to soften. Place one-sixth of the filling in the center of the tortilla and top with 1/4 cup of sauce. Fold in both sides of the tortilla to enclose the filling, and place seam-side down in an individual-serving-size oval gratin dish. (Alternatively, place all six wrapped tortillas in a 9 x 13 inch baking dish.)

10. Top each tortilla with 1/2 cup of sauce. Place dishes or baking pan in the preheated oven and bake until heated through, about 15 minutes.

11. Remove from oven and top each enchilada with 1/4 cup shredded mozzarella (optional) and garnish with cilantro before serving.

Salmon

Salmon is full of good-for-you DHA and relatively low in bad-for-you mercury. Wild salmon is a better choice due to lower levels of PCBs—another bad-for-you chemical—than in farmed fish.

Get the facts - pg. 106

Soy & Sesame Wild Salmon

About the blogger

Ambitious Deliciousness - http://www.ambitiousdeliciousness.com

Esther Chai
@ambitiousdelish

Growing up in South Korea, Esther's earliest memories include watching her mom cook in the kitchen. Esther was a curious little girl that always asked her mom lots of questions about the cooking process. Why didn't her mom use any measuring tools? Why did she use gochujang (red pepper paste) instead of gochugaru (red pepper flakes)?

Esther's mom discovered a surprisingly discerning palette in her six-year-old girl. As a result, she often allowed Esther to taste her food during the cooking process and made adjustments that way.

Like many people, Esther always equated home cooking with love. A delicious homemade meal is more than just food; it's love. It's a great way to show how much you care for those you are cooking for! Ambitious Deliciousness was born in 2008 as a result of Esther wanting to share her adventurous recipes with the rest of the world. She enjoys eating a variety of ethnic foods, coming up with new recipes, as well as recreating old ones with an unexpected twist.

Soy & Sesame Wild Salmon

Serves 2

1½ lbs wild salmon fillet

1 Tbsp soy sauce

1 Tbsp brown sugar

1 tsp rice vinegar

1 tsp sesame oil

1 Tbsp roasted sesame seeds

1 tsp freshly grated ginger

2 tsps canola oil

1 scallion, chopped (for garnish)

1. In a bowl, mix together soy sauce, brown sugar, rice vinegar, sesame oil, grated ginger, and sesame seeds with 2 tablespoons water.

2. Put salmon in a lidded container and pour 2/3 of the marinade mixture into the container. Reserve remaining marinade. Close the lid and shake gently, making sure the marinade has covered entire salmon. Place in refrigerator for 30 minutes.

3. Heat frying pan coated with canola oil over high heat. Add salmon and lower the heat to medium. Cook for 5–6 minutes, until salmon is no longer translucent. Flip with tongs and continue cooking the other side, for another 5 minutes.

4. Pour remaining marinade into the pan. Cook over low heat until sauce has evaporated.

5. Remove from pan and serve with chopped scallions on top.

Chicken

Chicken offers multiple nutrients with evidence for brain health—including choline, vitamin B6, and vitamin B12. While studies are less direct than on the DHA in coldwater fish, they suggest a benefit.

Get the facts - pg. 106

Murgh Malai Tikka Kabab

About the blogger

eCurry - http://www.ecurry.com/blog

Soma Rathore
@Soma_R

Soma grew up in a family that shared an excitement for cooking and entertaining. The little flame for the love of food was ignited in her heart. Her blog, which started off as a food journal, has gradually evolved as a canvas for her everyday experiences and discoveries in the kitchen, featuring home-cooked meals for her family and friends. The thrill in her kitchen is derived from the challenge of cooking nutritious, delicious, and varied food while she fuses the authentic Indian with international cuisine.

Murgh Malai Tikka Kabab

Makes 4-6 skewers

1 lb boneless chicken breast cut into
 ½ inch cubes

2 Tbsp ghee/clarified butter
 (can substitute butter)

½ lemon or lime, cut into wedges

½ onion, thickly sliced

Wet marinade

1 Tbsp shredded or crumbled
 mozzarella cheese

1 Tbsp lime juice

2 Tbsps heavy cream

1 Tbsp garlic paste

1 Tbsp onion, grated

2 Tbsps sour cream or Greek yogurt

1½ Tbsps ginger paste

1 Tbsp ghee/clarified butter
 (can substitute butter)

Dry marinade

¼ tsp meat tenderizer

Generous pinch saffron

1 tsp cumin seeds

1 tsp garam masala

Chili powder or cayenne pepper to taste (optional)

1 Tbsp kasoori methi (dried fenugreek leaves)
 or your favorite herb

1 Tbsp freshly ground black pepper

Sea salt

1. Wash chicken cubes and pat dry with a paper towel to remove as much moisture as you can.

2. In a bowl, combine all of the dry marinade ingredients and rub the mixture on to the chicken pieces. Chill chicken in refrigerator for about 30 minutes.

3. Mix all the ingredients for the wet marinade in a bowl or blender until you have a smooth paste. Add the wet marinade to the chicken pieces and toss to coat. Cover and place in the refrigerator for 1–2 hours.

4. While chicken is marinating, soak several wooden skewers in water for at least 30 minutes so they won't burn.

5. Remove the skewers from the water. Rub some marinade on each skewer and skewer the chicken with lime or lemon wedges and slices of onion.

6. If using a barbecue grill: heat barbecue and grill the skewers on one side. Turn and brush with marinade and ghee and continue cooking. If using a broiler: baste chicken with marinade and ghee and cook skewers about 20–25 minutes, until cooked through.

7. Remove from grill and serve immediately.

Ocean Trout Ingredient

Ocean Trout with Broccolini & Lemon

Serves 4

3 bunches broccolini
(or 2 heads broccoli)

Juice and zest of 1 lemon

2 Tbsps extra virgin olive oil plus
enough to season the trout

4 ocean trout fillets
(approximately 7 oz each)

Salt and pepper

2 lemons, cut in half

1. Bring a large pot of salted water to a boil. Cook broccolini for 3–4 minutes or until just tender. Drain and toss with lemon juice, lemon zest and 2 tablespoons olive oil. Season with salt and pepper, set aside, and keep warm.

2. Preheat a large frying pan or BBQ grill over medium-high heat. Rub trout fillets generously with olive oil and season well with salt and pepper on both sides.

3. Cook trout skin-side down for 3–4 minutes. Flip trout fillets over and add lemon halves to the pan, cut-side down. Sear trout on this side for another 3–4 minutes or until cooked to your liking.

4. Divide broccolini between four plates. Top with a trout fillet and add a seared lemon half on each plate.

*Trout

Omega 3 fatty acids—found in coldwater fish like trout—have multiple health benefits. In addition to showing promise for the prevention of psychotic disorders and cognitive impairments, they may help prevent certain cancers and cardiovascular disease.

Get the facts - pg. 106

About the blogger

stonesoup - http://thestonesoup.com/blog

Jules Clancy
@jules_stonesoup

Jules Clancy is a food scientist, photographer, writer, runner and aspiring minimalist. She lives in the beautiful city of Sydney. In January 2010, she packed in her day job as a chocolate biscuit designer for Australia's largest biscuit company to become a full-time blogger. She recently self-published her first cookbook, *and the love is free* which is available exclusively though her blog, stonesoup.

Quick Italian Tuna and Olive Pasta

Quick Italian Tuna & Olive Pasta

Serves 4

2 5-6 oz cans or jars of Italian tuna packed in olive oil

½ cup pitted olives, sliced

1½ cups cannellini beans, rinsed

2 tsps lemon juice

Zest of half a medium lemon

2 Tbsps parsley, finely chopped

2 Tbsps celery leaves, finely chopped

½ tsp crushed red pepper flakes

3 Tbsps extra virgin olive oil, divided

½ lb spaghetti

Salt to taste

1. In a large bowl, combine tuna with its oil, sliced olives, beans, lemon juice, lemon zest, parsley, celery leaves, and red pepper flakes. Add 1 1/2 tablespoons of extra virgin olive oil and lightly toss until well combined.

2. Cook pasta in a large pot of boiling salted water, uncovered, until al dente.

3. Drain and return to the pot. Add the tuna mixture to the pot and toss well. Add remaining 1 1/2 tablespoons of olive oil and lightly toss until pasta is well coated.

4. Warm until just heated through. Season with salt to taste.

5. Garnish with additional chopped fresh parsley, and drizzle with extra virgin olive oil. Serve immediately.

*Tuna

If you're going for canned tuna, keep in mind that white has almost three times as much DHA as light. DHA is a powerful brain food, with more evidence backing up its brain-healthy benefits than almost any other nutrient.

Get the facts - pg. 106

About the blogger

Food Blogga - http://foodblogga.blogspot.com

Susan Russo
@FoodBlogga

Susan Russo is a food writer and recipe developer in San Diego. She is a regular contributor to NPR's Kitchen Window and the founder of the popular cooking blog, Food Blogga. Her work has also been featured in Cooking Light. She is author of two cookbooks, *Recipes Every Man Should Know* and *The Encyclopedia of Sandwiches* (Quirk Books, fall/winter 2010). When she isn't writing about her Italian family in Rhode Island or life with her husband in Southern California, she can be found milling around a local farmers' market buying a lot more food than two people could possibly eat.

Sage Ingredient

Mustard & Sage Grilled Pork Tenderloin

Serves 2-4

1 pork tenderloin

Splash white wine vinegar

2 heaping Tbsps Dijon mustard

2 heaping tsps ground sage

1 clove garlic, minced

3 Tbsps canola oil

10 fresh sage leaves

Salt and pepper (lots)

1. Whisk together the mustard, sage, garlic, vinegar and canola oil in a bowl. Add salt and pepper to taste.

2. Place pork tenderloin in a dish, coat with mustard mixture, and marinate for 30 minutes to an hour.

3. Heat barbeque grill over high heat. Grease grill and place tenderloin directly on grill.

4. On the side facing up, place 5 sage leaves face down and press into meat. Cook on high for approximately 4 minutes, then flip tenderloin over.

5. Turn heat down to medium and line second side of the tenderloin with remaining sage leaves face down.

6. Continue cooking, turning occasionally until the interior of the tenderloin reads 155 degrees F.

7. Remove from heat, cover, and let rest for 10 minutes. Slice and serve.

*Sage

Studies have shown that the humble sage leaf, or its extracts, can improve your mood, boost your short-term memory, and help you pay attention better.

Get the facts - pg. 106

About the blogger

Daily Unadventures in Cooking - http://www.dailyunadventuresincooking.com

Katerina Wright
@dailyuncooking

Katerina is the creator of Daily Unadventures in Cooking, a food blog written for the home cook featuring simple recipes. Originally started as a way to document and learn to cook, it chronicles her journey as she learns a few new things, creates recipes, and has a disaster or two. All recipes and opinions are served up with a pinch of spice and a touch of sarcasm.

Katerina works full time in the software industry and is about to embark on a new adventure—4 months of culinary school! She is based in Vancouver but likes to run away to the country to cook incredibly local ingredients and work on her vegetable garden.

Rob's Favorite Lamb Kofta

Rob's Favorite Lamb Kofta

Makes 12 skewers

1 medium onion, cut into 8 wedges

2 garlic cloves, roughly chopped

¼ tsp cinnamon

½ tsp turmeric

¼ tsp chili powder

1 tsp cumin

½ tsp salt

¼ tsp freshly ground pepper

1 egg, lightly beaten

1 cup bread crumbs

1 lb ground lamb

1. Put the onion wedges and chopped garlic in a food processor and pulse until the onion is chopped into small pieces.

2. Add the cinnamon, turmeric, chili powder, cumin, salt, and pepper, and process until combined.

3. Add the egg, bread crumbs, and ground lamb and process until a sticky paste is formed, scraping down the bowl as necessary.

4. Form about a third of a cup of the lamb mixture around each skewer to cover the top third of the skewer. Refrigerate the skewers for 20 minutes to help them hold their shape.

5. Heat a grill pan or BBQ and cook the skewers for 5–6 minutes on each side until cooked through. If desired, serve with tzatziki sauce.

*Lamb

Lamb is a great source of dietary niacin, which studies suggest may offer protection from degenerative brain diseases.

Get the facts - pg. 106

About the blogger

Apples and Butter - http://www.applesandbutter.com

Jessica Durff
@ApplesandButter

Jessica created her first recipe at the age of four. It was a recipe for chocolate chip bread that included more sugar than flour. Her kind family sampled the bread, but Jessica didn't create much of anything else in the kitchen for the next fifteen years. While in college, she tried her hand at cooking once again and this time, fell in love.

Today, Jessica writes the award-winning food blog Apples and Butter. She spends her spare time perusing farmers' markets and digging in the soil in her backyard in an effort to procure the freshest and most delicious produce. While Jessica often takes a healthy approach to food, she believes that puff pastry and butter have an important place in every kitchen.

*Chicken

Not many meats have proven benefits for the brain. Most "brain foods" are vegetables, fruits, or fish. But chicken has several nutrients that may promote brain health—including choline and B vitamins.

Get the facts - pg. 106

Slow Roast Stuffed Chicken

About the blogger

Greedy Gourmet - http://www.greedygourmet.com

Michelle Minnaar
@tweetygourmet

Michelle Minnaar, a.k.a. Greedy Gourmet, fell in love with an Englishman and left South Africa to live with him in the UK. She discovered that they were surrounded by a plethora of terrible restaurants that served pricy food that was mediocre at best. She donned her apron and that was that. Along the way Michelle discovered her passion for photography and is hoping to become a freelance food and travel photographer in the next few years when given the opportunity. At the moment she is a full time mother to two little connoisseurs who love duck pâté, smoked salmon and condensed milk. She also set up an online cookware shop (http://shop.greedygourmet.com), selling only the highest quality kitchen gear she can get a hold of and has tested thoroughly.

Slow Roast Stuffed Chicken

Serves 4-6

¼ cup butter, divided

1 onion, chopped

1 tsp ground allspice

⅓ cup basmati rice

⅓ cup pecans, chopped

2 Tbsps pine nuts

½ cup sultanas [golden raisins]

½ cup + ⅔ cup
    chicken stock, divided

1 whole 5 lb chicken

¼ tsp freshly ground black pepper

½ tsp salt

1. Put 2 tablespoons butter into a large frying pan and melt it over medium heat. Add the onion and cook for 5 minutes until the onion is translucent and soft. Stir in the allspice.

2. Add the rice and nuts to the pan, and then cook for 2–3 minutes over medium-high heat. Add the sultanas, 1/2 cup of chicken stock and 1/4 cup of water. Bring to boil, then reduce the heat and simmer for 8–10 minutes, until the water is absorbed. Set aside to cool.

3. Preheat the oven to 285 degrees F. Rinse the cavity of the chicken with cold water and pat dry inside and out with paper towels.

4. Spoon cooled stuffing into the cavity. Truss the chicken with string, then place in a deep baking dish. Rub salt and pepper into the skin with your fingertips.

5. Melt remaining 2 tablespoons of butter and pour over the chicken, then add remaining 2/3 cup stock to the pan. Roast for 2 hours and 30 minutes, basting every 30 minutes with juices from the pan.

6. Increase the oven's temperature to 350 degrees F, and cook for 30 minutes more to brown the chicken thoroughly.

Salmon Ingredient

Garlic Salmon over Spinach

Serves 4

4 4 oz salmon fillets

2 Tbsps butter

6 garlic cloves, minced, divided

2 tsps lemon pepper seasoning

6 oz fresh spinach

1. Melt butter in a large skillet over medium-high heat.

2. Stir in 4 cloves of minced garlic.

3. Sprinkle salmon fillets on both sides with lemon pepper seasoning.

4. Place the salmon in the pan and cook on both sides for approximately 3–5 minutes per side, until fish flakes when tested with a fork.

5. Meanwhile, steam fresh spinach for about 4 minutes, or until tender.

6. Toss spinach with remaining 2 cloves of minced garlic.

7. Serve the salmon fillets over the spinach.

*Salmon

You've probably heard that omega-3s, especially the DHA in salmon, are good for your brain—with good reason. They've been shown to protect brain health in newborns, improve cognitive performance in adults, and prevent or ameliorate age-related cognitive decline.

Get the facts - pg. 106

About the blogger

Dine & Dish - http://www.dineanddish.net

Kristen Doyle
@dineanddish

At Dine & Dish, freelance writer Kristen Doyle chronicles her culinary adventures in a fun, family-friendly environment. Kristen's mission is to help others make family mealtime a priority, where families gather around the table each night to engage in great food and conversation. As a mom of 4 kids under the age of 8, Kristen understands how important family mealtime can be. With recipes that are quick and simple to get on the table, Dine & Dish is a resource for anyone looking to simplify their lives in order to reconnect with their family, one meal at a time.

*Garlic

Bad breath = good brain! Garlic
has been shown improve memory
and cognitive performance in
healthy and impaired subjects,
and may help to stave off
Alzheimer's. It also has strong
antioxidant properties.

Get the facts - pg. 106

Garlic Ingredient

About the blogger

Eclectic Recipes - http://eclecticrecipes.com

Angelia McGowan
@EclecticRecipes

Angelia's interpretation of southern cooking is much different than
the perception of southern cuisine today. She uses a lot of fresh
fruits, vegetables and smaller portions of meat; and doesn't deep-
fry everything in sight! This is the type of cooking that Angelia
was raised on. She had an abundance of vegetables from local farm
crops, but meats were always served sparingly because of cost.
Angelia has continued this traditional way of cooking with her
own family and also added more healthy habits to her cooking.
She cooks with only whole food ingredients, whole grains
whenever possible and uses lots of olive oil.

Balsamic Roasted Garlic Chicken with Angel Hair Pasta

Serves 4

16 oz angel hair pasta

2 whole heads of garlic

2 cups balsamic vinegar

4 oz jar of pimentos

4 boneless skinless chicken breasts

Olive oil

Kosher salt

1. Preheat oven to 400 degrees F.

2. Take a head of garlic and remove as much of the outer skins as possible while leaving the head intact. Cut off the top end of the head of garlic, about 1/4 - 1/2 inch, so that the inner cloves are exposed. Repeat with the other head of garlic.

3. Place each head of garlic in aluminum foil. Drizzle the top of the garlic with olive oil and a little kosher salt. Wrap garlic up in the aluminum foil tightly and place the heads of garlic in a baking pan. Roast garlic in a 400 degrees F oven for approximately 30 minutes, or until very fragrant and soft.

4. Season chicken with salt and pepper. Preheat a large skillet over high heat. Brown chicken on both sides.

5. Cook pasta according to package directions.

6. When chicken is fully cooked, remove from pan and set aside. Add balsamic vinegar and the jar of pimentos with their juice. Squeeze the roasted garlic out of the cloves and add to the pan. Smash cloves with a fork and simmer until the sauce has reduced by about 1/4.

7. Add chicken back to pan and continue to simmer until sauce has reduced by about 1/2 and has thickened.

8. Serve chicken and sauce over pasta.

Chocolate and Banana Ingredients

Chocolate Banana Milkshake

Serves 1

⅓ cup raw almonds

1 tsp honey

1 Tbsp dark cocoa powder

1 ripe banana

10 ice cubes

1. Soak the almonds in a bowl filled with water for at least 6 hours or overnight.

2. Drain almonds and place them in a blender.

3. Add 1 cup water. Blend on high for a minute or two until the almonds are chopped very finely.

4. Add honey, banana, cocoa powder, and ice cubes. Blend for 1 additional minute until smooth.

5. Drink immediately.

*Banana

Bananas may not be a major brain food, but they do offer a significant dose of vitamins B6 and C—both of which may promote better brain health. Plus, the chocolate in this milkshake adds an extra brain boost! **Get the facts - pg. 106**

About the blogger

Laurel on Health Food - http://www.laurelonhealthfood.com

Laurel Moll
@LaurelMoll

Blogging about healthy food and nutrition started out as a hobby for Laurel, but it quickly became a full-time gig. Laurel is a holistic health coach, and loves to talk about food! She grew up in a family with some wonderful cooks, but it wasn't until Laurel moved out on her own that she realized how much she enjoyed cooking and dreaming up her own recipes. For her, eating healthy is fulfilling and fun, and blogging gives her a chance to share that with her clients and readers. Since chocolate is one of her favorite foods on the planet, she knew she had to share her Chocolate Banana Milkshake recipe.

Blueberries

Blueberries are a superpower in the world of antioxidants. Studies suggest that eating blueberries may protect against oxidative stress, improve memory, and prevent cognitive decline.

Get the facts - pg. 106

Blueberry Ingredient

About the blogger

the arugula files - http://www.arugulafiles.com

Mary Cunningham
@arugulafiles

Mary grew up on canned vegetables and processed foods. She's trying to kick the habit by visiting farmers' markets more often and cooking with whole ingredients. Basically, she's learning to eat better. Her blog, the arugula files, is about delicious food. Mary writes about her experiences learning to cook, eating out, collecting cookbooks, her addiction to the Food Network, and how she manages to cook anything in her tiny kitchen. Some original recipes from her collection include rhubarb pop-tarts, pizza with peaches and arugula, and mushroom and shallot pie.

Blueberry & Crème Fraîche Ice Cream

Serves 4

3 cups fresh blueberries

½ cup sugar

8 oz crème fraîche

1. Clean blueberries and place in a stainless steel pan over medium heat. Add sugar. Bring to rolling boil, stirring constantly, and then turn heat to low.

2. Cook on low heat for about five minutes, or until blueberries are mostly liquid (there will be some remaining chunks of blueberries). Remove from heat, pour mixture into a bowl and place in fridge until cool, about 1 hour.

3. Remove blueberry mixture from fridge and mix in crème fraîche.

Directions with an Ice Cream Maker

1. Pour blueberry crème fraîche mixture into ice cream maker, following machine instructions.

Directions without an Ice Cream Maker

1. Pour ice cream mixture into a chilled wide-lipped, deep bowl (ceramic or stainless steel is best) and place in fridge for about 1 hour. Remove from fridge and place in freezer.

2. After 30 minutes check on the mixture. It should be starting to freeze around the edges. Stir the ice cream until it is creamy again and then put it back in the freezer.

3. Repeat step 2 three more times, every 30 minutes. Store in freezer in covered container until ready to serve.

Banana Oatmeal Chocolate Chip Cookies

Banana Oatmeal Chocolate Chip Cookies

Makes 25 cookies

½ cup whole wheat flour

1 cup rolled oats (not instant)

½ tsp baking powder

½ tsp baking soda

¼ tsp cinnamon

1 Tbsp ground flaxseed meal

¼ cup agave nectar

¼ cup soy milk (can substitute regular milk)

½ tsp vanilla extract

1 Tbsp canola oil

1 ripe banana

½ cup dark chocolate chips

¼ cup walnuts, chopped

1. Preheat oven to 350 degrees F.

2. Combine all ingredients in a large bowl. Mix well until batter is blended evenly.

3. Use a tablespoon to portion cookies on a greased baking sheet, approximately 1–2 inches apart.

4. Bake cookies for 12–15 minutes.

5. Remove cookies from baking sheet and allow to cool on wire rack.

*Chocolate, Banana, Flax, and Walnuts

What makes these cookies good for the brain? They benefit from a combination of brain foods: chocolate, banana, flax, and walnuts. The more brain-healthy ingredients, the better!

Get the facts - pg. 106

About the blogger

Carrots 'N' Cake - http://carrotsncake.com

Tina Haupert
@carrotsncake

Tina loves food, and loves to eat! While she tries to fill her diet with mostly healthy foods, Tina has a number of favorites that are not necessarily nutritious, but are still delicious and fun to eat. If eaten in moderation, she believes that the "bad" foods can be part of an overall healthy diet. This food philosophy is the inspiration for her blog as well as these Banana Oatmeal Chocolate Chip Cookies.

Açaí Mousse - Photo Courtesy Rita Turner

Açaí Mousse

Serves 10

1 package (0.25 oz) unflavored gelatin

1¼ cups frozen açaí pulp, thawed

2 egg whites, room temperature

4½ Tbsps agave nectar

1 cup whipping cream, chilled

1 tsp vanilla extract

Cooking spray

1. Dissolve the gelatin in 1/2 cup of boiling water.

2. In a small saucepan, bring the açaí pulp to a boil and let it reduce for 5 minutes. The pulp will thicken slightly.

3. In a large bowl, mix the açaí pulp with the dissolved gelatin. Set aside to cool.

4. Beat the egg whites with a mixer until soft peaks form. Continue beating while slowly drizzling the agave nectar into the egg whites. Turn off mixer when eggs have reached a stiff meringue (beaters hold stiff peaks). Using a rubber spatula, gently fold the egg whites into the açaí gelatin.

5. In a separate bowl, beat the cream and vanilla until you reach soft peaks. Gently fold the whipped cream with the açaí and egg white mixture until there are no streaks of white in the mousse.

6. Spray an 8-inch round cake pan or a bundt pan with cooking spray and scrape mousse into pan. Cover with plastic wrap and refrigerate for at least 6 hours or overnight.

7. To serve, dip the bottom of the pan in hot water and carefully unmold it onto a plate.

*Açaí

While the jury is still out on açaí's benefits for the brain, early studies in mice show it might help stave off certain forms of dementia. More studies are in progress.

Get the facts - pg. 106

About the blogger

Pink Bites - http://www.pinkbites.com

Rita Turner

Born in Brazil and living in the Pacific Northwest, Rita believes cooking is much more than preparing food, it's a nurturing act. "For me, cooking has healed many wounds and opened many doors." Her fresh and simple cooking is influenced by her Brazilian background as well as her many travels around the world. She finds her happy place in the kitchen and behind the lenses of her camera. Rita's recipes and photography can be seen on her blog Pink Bites.

*Dark Chocolate

Flavanols, the compounds
in dark chocolate that have
been associated with cognitive
health, are also found in other
delicious treats: red wine and
coffee are good sources, too.

Get the facts - pg. 106

Dark Chocolate Covered Strawberry Tart

About the blogger

Local Appetite - http://www.localappetiteny.com

Jen Bernstein
@localappetite

Jen is a food obsessed girl from Queens, who moved to Manhattan, and did short stints in Madrid, Spain and Atlanta, Georgia before happily settling (for now) in Brooklyn. Every place she has lived has influenced her tastes and expanded her views on food. No other author has influenced her thoughts and beliefs as much as Michael Pollan. Jen was fortunate enough to grow up in a household where they always ate dinner together around six o'clock. Food was very important and they never skimped on it, but it was rarely made from scratch. Cooking was a chore, not for fun. As an adult, Jen couldn't disagree more. Cooking makes her happy, while baking puts a smile to Jen's face and makes her forget about any troubles. While she was in school Jen worked in many front of the house positions and after law school did a brief stagiere in the pastry department at Eleven Madison Park. Her at-home cooking philosophy is to buy the best ingredients she can afford, and whenever possible support local businesses and purveyors. If it's grown near by, that's her first choice. This doesn't mean she is about to give up lemons and avocados because she lives in the Northeast. Jen started Local Appetite to learn about the ingredients that are local to her region, but also as a journal for the things that she creates in her kitchen, as she believes homemade is always best.

Dark Chocolate Covered Strawberry Tart

Serves 7-8

Chocolate Tart Dough

1 cup minus 2 Tbsps unbleached
all-purpose flour

2 Tbsps + 2 tsps cocoa powder

½ cup unsalted butter, room temperature,
cut into 8 pieces

½ cup + 2 Tbsps powdered sugar

1 egg yolk

Dark Chocolate Topping

6½ oz high quality dark chocolate
(70% preferable), chopped

¾ cup light cream

1 egg yolk

Extra dark chocolate for shavings on top
for decoration

Strawberry Filling

½ cup strawberry jam

2 baskets of strawberries, sliced (or enough
to cover bottom of tart shell)

Chocolate Tart Dough

1. Sift together flour and the cocoa powder. Set aside.

2. Cream butter and powdered sugar in a stand mixer or with a hand-held mixer. When well-beaten, add the egg yolk and beat until blended. Add half the flour/cocoa mixture and beat in until it becomes crumbly. Add the remaining flour/cocoa and mix in just until dough holds together.

3. Form dough into a disc and wrap in plastic wrap. Chill in the refrigerator for at least 2 hours or up to overnight.

4. Remove dough from refrigerator and roll out the dough between two sheets of plastic wrap to 1/8 inch thickness. If it crumbles, just press it back together. (The plastic wrap should help it stay together as you roll.)

5. Gently place dough in a tart pan, and use your fingertips to press the sides into the bottom to make sure it is well fitted. Using your rolling pin, roll over the top of the tart shell to cut off any excess dough and give you a neat edge. Prick all over the base of the dough with a fork. Place in the freezer for 10–15 minutes.

6. Preheat oven to 375 degrees F. Bake chilled tart until crust is dry to the touch, about 15 minutes. Let cool while you make the chocolate cream.

Dark Chocolate Topping

1. Place the chopped chocolate and cream in a saucepan and cook over a low heat, stirring, until chocolate has melted. Remove from the heat and beat in the egg yolk with a whisk. Set aside.

To Assemble the Tart

1. Spread a layer of strawberry jam inside the cooled tart shell.

2. Lay strawberry slices on top of the jam and cover the base of the tart. Try to keep them in a single layer, without piling them up too high.

3. Pour the chocolate cream over the strawberries and smooth out with a knife or spatula. Decorate the top with a few strawberry slices in the middle and shavings of dark chocolate (if using).

4. Chill in the refrigerator until chocolate cream has firmed, about one hour.

Sweet Potatoes

Orange vegetables get their color from beta carotene—a powerful antioxidant. Some studies suggest that a low level of beta carotene is associated with poorer cognitive function, especially in older adults.

Get the facts - pg. 106

Sweet Potato Bread Pudding with Maple Pecan Crunch

About the blogger

Dixie Caviar - http://www.dixiecaviar.com

Nealey Dozier
@dixiecaviar

Nealey moved from Alabama to the West Coast to follow her dreams, only to realize once there how much she missed good ol' country cooking. So she took to the kitchen and began recreating the dishes of her past, but this time without any help from a can. What started out as a hobby turned into an obsession, so she quit her day job to pursue cooking – and eating – full time. Dixie Caviar is where you can follow her pursuits of all things Southern.

Sweet Potato Bread Pudding with Maple Pecan Crunch

Serves 8-10

2 large sweet potatoes, about 1 lb each

1 (16 ounce) loaf day-old soft
bread, cut into 1 inch cubes
(Challah bread is best)

2 cups whole milk

2 eggs

2 egg whites

¾ cup brown sugar, packed

½ tsp vanilla extract

½ tsp cinnamon

Maple Pecan Crunch

2 cups pecan halves

¼ cup pure maple syrup

1 tsp bourbon (optional)

Whiskey Sauce

½ cup unsalted butter

¼ cup sugar

1 egg, lightly beaten

1 Tbsp bourbon (optional)

1. Preheat oven to 400 degrees F.

2. Prick each sweet potato a few times with a fork. Place on a baking sheet and bake in oven until soft, approximately one hour and fifteen minutes. Allow to cool, then remove skins and transfer sweet potatoes to a large bowl. Mash with a potato masher or fork.

3. Add milk, eggs, egg whites, brown sugar, vanilla, and cinnamon to sweet potatoes. Whisk until well combined. Fold in bread cubes.

4. Pour bread mixture into a greased 9 x 13 pan and smooth top. Cover and chill for 2 hours in the refrigerator.

Maple Pecan Crunch

1. Stir together pecans, maple syrup, and bourbon in a large bowl. Spread on a baking sheet lined with parchment paper and cook 12–14 minutes, stirring every 5 minutes and watching carefully that they don't burn.

2. Remove from oven and move parchment paper to a cool surface. Allow pecans to cool, stirring frequently so they don't stick together. Coarsely chop.

Whiskey Sauce

1. In a double boiler (or a bowl set over simmering water), melt butter and sugar and whisk until sugar is dissolved, about 10 minutes.

2. Remove from heat and whisk in egg, stirring vigorously to prevent egg from curdling.

3. Stir in bourbon.

To Bake and Serve

1. Remove bread pudding from refrigerator and bake at 400 degrees F until firm and lightly browned, approximately 35–40 minutes.

2. Sprinkle pecan mixture on top, pressing in gently to secure. Serve warm with whiskey sauce.

Pomegranate

Ahhh, pomegranate. Beautiful, pink, and brain-healthy. Like olive oil, pomegranate is a rich source of polyphenols, which may protect the brains of unborn babies and people at risk of Alzheimer's.

Get the facts - pg. 106

Pomegranate Ingredient

About the blogger

Off The (Meat) Hook - http://www.offthemeathook.com

Karen Merzenich
@offthemeathook

Karen lives in San Francisco where she was born and raised. A professionally trained pastry chef, she has at various times held almost every single job in a restaurant, from coat check to line cook to server to pastry chef. She now works in another area of passion—neuroscience. While exceedingly glad to have hung up her toque professionally, she still loves cooking, inventing, enjoying, and sharing.

Seductive Strawberry Pomegranate Pie

Serves 8

1½ cups flour

½ cup vegetable shortening
or butter

3-4 Tbsps ice cold milk or water

4 cups strawberries, sliced

Seeds from 1 pomegranate

3 Tbsps cornstarch

¼-½ cup sugar

1¾ cups pure unsweetened
pomegranate juice

Pinch of salt

1. Preheat oven to 375 degrees F.

2. Combine flour, salt, and shortening or butter with a pastry blender, your fingers, a fork, or a food processor, until pastry pieces are about the size of lentils.

3. Add 2 tablespoons milk or water and mix gently to combine. Add more liquid little by little as necessary to create a dough that's tender and well-combined, but not wet or sticky.

4. Form dough into a ball and wrap in plastic wrap. Chill for 30 minutes.

5. Remove dough from refrigerator. Using a rolling pin, roll the crust out on a floured surface to 1/4 inch thickness and place in a pie pan. Press into corners and over top of pie pan, then trim excess dough.

6. Poke holes on bottom and sides with a fork. Bake for about 20 minutes, until crust is lightly browned. Remove from oven and cool.

7. Meanwhile, combine cornstarch, 1/4 cup sugar, and pomegranate juice in a saucepan and stir with a whisk. Heat over medium heat and bring to a boil. Boil for 1 minute, stirring constantly. Remove from heat.

8. Check the glaze's sweetness by dipping a strawberry slice in and tasting it. If it's too tart, add more sugar and stir in while glaze is still warm. Set aside to cool.

9. When glaze is room temperature, stir the strawberries and 3/4 of the pomegranate seeds in. Pour into cooled pie crust and sprinkle remaining pomegranate seeds on top.

10. Chill in fridge for at least four hours to set the glaze. Serve chilled with a dollop of whipped cream or ice cream.

Dark Chocolate Ingredient

Superfood Fudge Pops

Makes 6-8 pops

½ cup coconut milk

3½ oz dark chocolate, finely chopped

11 oz açaí juice

⅓ cup agave nectar

Pinch of salt

1. Place the dark chocolate into a bowl and set aside.

2. On the stove, heat the coconut milk in a small pot for about 1–2 minutes, until just on the brink of boiling. Pour the heated coconut milk over the chocolate. Let sit for a few minutes to allow the chocolate to melt, then stir well, until completely smooth.

3. Pour in the açaí juice, agave nectar, and salt, and mix thoroughly to combine.

4. Let cool to room temperature, and pour into pop molds. Place in the freezer and allow at least 4 hours before serving, or until the pops are completely solid.

*Dark Chocolate

When it comes to the brain, the darker the chocolate the better. Darker chocolate has a higher flavanol content.

Get the facts - pg. 106

About the blogger

BitterSweet - http://www.bittersweetblog.com

Hannah Kaminsky
@bittersweet__

Hannah Kaminsky is a dedicated vegan baker, blogger, photographer and crafter. Her first cookbook, "My Sweet Vegan: Passionate about Dessert," was published in 2007, when Hannah was still in high school. For over four years, she has written the popular Bittersweetblog.com that showcases her newest recipe creations, crafts and photographs, with occasional cookbook and new product reviews. She has also published five e-books of themed vegan recipes. In her spare time, Hannah is working toward a degree in commercial photography and works part-time at Health in a Hurry, a local healthy food restaurant.

Hannah always makes it a point to shop at local farms and greenmarkets whenever possible. She loves to travel, and no vacation is complete without a trip to every local supermarket and produce stand she can find, along with a pick-your-own farm if time and season allows.

Photography is another way for Hannah to express her creativity. Starting with a few classes in high school, she has learned techniques and sensibilities from mentors and teachers, and continues to learn and practice almost daily. Her food photographs have been published in numerous cookbooks and magazines. After she attains her photography degree, she hopes to work in this field more steadily.

Flaxseed

Ground flaxseed has little flavor, and can be added to many recipes (desserts and other dishes) for a brain-health benefit. It contains a high concentration of ALA, an omega-3 fatty acid.

Get the facts - pg. 106

Cardamom flaxseed thumbprint cookies

About the blogger

make life sweeter! - http://linda.kovacevic.nl

Linda Kovacevic

Back in the 70's Linda's parents believed that minimizing sugar intake was the best for children (which of course it is). But her parents went further than most by restricting sugary things to birthdays and the like. Sugar-free licorice was a treat for Linda and her brother. Their regime seemed to have been working and for years she was really was more of a savory girl than a sweet girl. But about 7 years this started to change. At the time she and her boyfriend were living in Tel Aviv, Israel. There they would eat out a lot and enjoy the wonderfully delicious foods in the restaurants. Contrary to what they were used to in The Netherlands (where they're from) the desserts were very good—so good that she changed her usual habit of ordering appetizers and main course to main course and dessert. Inspired by those desserts, she started baking more and more at home until one day she discovered there was such a thing as a food blog. And before Linda knew it she started her own. Her eldest son was about 5 months old at the time. In the 4+ years that she has had her blog, her two other sons were born and they moved back to The Hague, The Netherlands and since June last year Linda, her sons, and their father have relocated to Vienna, Austria, enjoying every bit of their sweet life.

Cardamom Flaxseed Thumbprint Cookies

Makes 20 cookies

½ cup flour + 2 Tbsps flour

5 Tbsps flaxseed, ground

6 Tbsps powdered sugar

½ tsp cardamom, powdered

1 stick butter, softened

1 Tbsp sour cream

3 Tbsps kumquat marmalade (recipe follows—can substitute store-bought orange marmalade)

Kumquat Marmalade

7 oz kumquats, cut into wedges, seeds removed

1 ½ cups orange juice

½ oz pectin mix (for 18 oz fruit)

2 ½ cups sugar

1. Sift together flour and powdered sugar. Add flaxseed and cardamom. Add butter and sour cream and mix by hand with a spoon or in a machine, until just combined, without overmixing. Form the dough into a ball and let it rest in the refrigerator for 1/2 hour.

2. Preheat the oven 350 degrees F. Grease a baking sheet.

3. Remove dough from refrigerator and divide it into 20 equal pieces. Roll each piece into a ball. Place balls onto greased baking sheet. Using your thumb or finger, make a deep impression in the center of each ball.

4. Bake for about 15 minutes or until slightly browned. Allow to cool on baking sheet for a few minutes before transferring to a wire rack to cool completely.

5. In a small pot over low heat, warm the marmalade with 1/2 teaspoon water and mix. Fill the cookies with hot marmalade. Allow to cool and set before eating.

6. Allow to cool and set.

Kumquat Marmalade

1. Place kumquat wedges in a saucepan and cover with cold water. Bring to a boil and cook until soft, about 15–20 minutes. Drain.

2. Process cooked kumquats in a food processor. Add orange juice a bit at a time, until you have approximately 2 cups of kumquat puree.

3. Pour the kumquat mixture into a large saucepan. Sprinkle the pectin mix into the saucepan and bring to a boil while stirring.

4. Add the sugar and bring to a boil, stirring constantly. Continue cooking for 10 minutes, still stirring. Remove from heat and cool to room temperature before using to fill the cookies.

Glossary

Açaí

Studies in rats have shown that frozen açaí pulp may have a positive contribution in the development of age-related neurodegenerative diseases, and may prevent oxidative damage in certain areas of the brain. *Reference: 1*

Almonds

Almonds are one of the most concentrated sources of vitamin E available. Vitamin E at a high daily dose has been shown to delay the progression of Alzheimer's disease, and vitamin E intake is generally associated with less age-related cognitive decline. In one study, participants who received vitamin E improved statistically and clinically in some memory and verbal measures, while participants who received a placebo did not improve. *Reference: 2*

Artichokes

Artichokes are rich in luteolin derivatives, a type of antioxidant flavanoid. Luteolin has been shown to have positive effects in a wide variety of cognitive issues, including enhancing memory in neurodegenerative disorders, protecting synaptic function, and potentially improving outcomes in Multiple Sclerosis (MS), autism, and Parkinson's disease. *Reference: 3*

Asparagus

Asparagus is an excellent source of vitamin A, vitamin C, and folic acid, all of which contribute to healthy cognitive functioning. Vitamin A has been shown to contribute to maintaining brain plasticity in adulthood. All three vitamins likely play an important role in cognition, and may have potential in the prevention of Alzheimer's disease. *References: 4, 6, 14*

Bananas

Bananas offer a significant daily intake of two key nutrients: vitamin B6 and vitamin C. Low intake of vitamin B6 has been associated with an increased risk of Parkinson's disease, while increasing intake of vitamin C has been shown to slow cognitive decline in older people, and may decrease stress and improve mood in healthy adults. *References: 5, 6*

Blueberries

Perhaps more than any other food, blueberries are associated with better brain health. Blueberries are a rich source of antioxidants and anti-inflammatories, making them a popular subject of studies on cognitive functioning. Many of these studies suggest that eating blueberries may protect against oxidative stress, improve memory and cognition, and prevent cognitive decline. However, as with other "brain foods," more study is needed to verify these benefits in humans. *Reference: 7*

Butternut Squash

Butternut squash is a winter squash, a category that also includes acorn, kabocha, spaghetti, and Hubbard squashes. Winter squashes are rich in beta-carotene, plus they boast a healthy dose of vitamin C, folic acid, niacin, and antioxidants, which also offer brain benefits—with a very low caloric load. *References: 6, 14, 17, 26*

Chicken

Chicken is a great source of lean protein, offers a balance of brain-healthy compounds, and is a good source of dietary choline and vitamins B6 and B12. Choline and the B vitamins have been shown to play important roles in healthy cognition and provide neuroprotective benefits. Choline is an essential building block in acetylcholine, a brain chemical that helps memory. *References: 5, 8, 13*

Cranberries

Cranberries have been identified as one of the most excellent dietary sources of high-quality antioxidants. Antioxidants have been shown to prevent and ameliorate oxidative stress in the brain and body and maintain healthy cognitive functioning. *References: 9, 10*

Dark chocolate

Cocoa is rich in flavonoids (sometimes called flavanols), compounds that have been linked to improved cognitive performance in older adults. Studies have shown that cocoa flavanols improve performance in healthy adults during sustained mental effort and may also protect against stroke. *Reference: 12*

Eggs

Eggs are rich in choline, a nutrient that has been associated with long-term memory development. Choline is also a key ingredient in the neurotransmitter acetylcholine (ACh), which is necessary for healthy neurotransmission. Studies have shown that choline intake promotes recovery from learning memory disorders in the aging brain, and may even improve psychic function in those with senile dementia or Alzheimer's. Egg yolks are also rich in omega-3 fatty acids, yielding additional brain benefits at a relatively low caloric cost. *References: 13, 14, 24*

Flaxseed

Flaxseeds are full of ALA, a type of omega-3 fatty acid that the body may be able to convert to the brain-benefitting DHA. They're also one of the best sources of lignans—an estrogen-like chemical. Studies on lignan intake and ground flaxseed consumption suggest that they have potential for improving cognitive performance, especially among postmenopausal women. One study showed that 40 grams of flaxseed a day cut hot flashes (caused when the brain's hypothalamus gets confused) by 50%, though a later study refutes that. *References: 30*

Garbanzo beans—Lentils—Split Peas

Legumes like garbanzo beans, lentils, and split peas are a rich source of folic acid. Studies have shown that folic acid can improve verbal and memory performance, and may delay onset of Alzheimer's disease. Getting enough folic acid while pregnant is important for fetal brain development too—especially in early pregnancy. It can help prevent neural tube defects—a leading cause of infant mortality in the U.S. and elsewhere. *Reference: 14*

Garlic

Garlic has been shown improve memory and cognitive performance in healthy and impaired subjects, and may help to stave off Alzheimer's. It also has strong antioxidant properties. *References: 10, 15*

Kiwifruit

Kiwis pack a significant vitamin C punch—nearly 100% of the recommended daily value in just one fruit. Vitamin C is essential for healthy cognition and may influence mood and stress. Kiwifruits are also an excellent source of multiple types of antioxidants, and as such may prevent oxidative stress in brain and body cells. *References: 6, 10, 16*

Lamb

Lamb is a rich source of niacin, which has been identified as one of the most important nutrients for optimal cognition and neuro-protection. A 9-year study of over 6,000 people aged 65 and over showed that regular intake of niacin-rich foods, such as lamb, may protect against Alzheimer's disease and age-related cognitive decline. Lamb is also rich in vitamin B12, which is key for nerve cell development. *References: 8, 17*

Oats

Oats are rich in selenium, an antioxidant that has been shown to have protective effects in a variety of brain disorders and age-related cognitive problems. They also supply a sustained energy source to the brain, which may help people learn better. A study of school children showed that those who ate oatmeal before school performed significantly better on spatial memory and auditory learning tasks than those who ate a sugar cereal. *Reference: 29*

Olive Oil

Olive oil is rich in polyphenols, a group of easily-absorbed chemicals with antioxidant and anti-inflammatory properties. A diet rich in polyphenols may suppress the onset of Alzheimer's by preventing oxidative damage, and because they chelate metals, their routine use may also be protective against the onset of Alzheimer's. Olive oil is also a good source of vitamin E, which has been shown to delay the progression of Alzheimer's disease, and which is generally associated with less age-related cognitive decline. Several observational studies on the brain benefits of the Mediterranean diet position olive oil consumption as one of the most important factors. *References: 2, 18*

Onions

Onions are rich in the antioxidant quercetin, which has been shown to protect against ischemic brain damage (a type of stroke) and may improve impaired memory. Quercetin has also been implicated as a potential anti-depressant. *Reference: 19*

Pomegranates

Pomegranates have been shown to have a host of brain-boosting compounds, including polyphenols and resveratrol, which have antioxidant and anti-aging effects in the brain. Early studies suggest that the compounds in pomegranates may be useful in treating Alzheimer's disease. Pomegranate juice has also been shown to protect the fetal brain. *Reference: 20*

Quinoa

Quinoa is a seed that's rich in all of the essential amino acids-especially lysine. Lysine may play a key role in regulating anxiety and stress. Studies have shown that those with a lysine deficiency manifest significantly elevated anxiety levels and higher concentrations of stress hormones. Quinoa also offers a large dose of magnesium, which has been demonstrated to reduce inflammation-related brain injury and lessen the brain's likelihood of hemorrhage. *References: 21, 22*

Sage

Sage has long been thought to have medicinal properties, and current science has borne that out. Administration of sage or sage extracts has been shown to improve memory, attention, and mood in healthy young adults, and may improve outcomes in Alzheimer's disease. *Reference: 23*

Salmon – Sardines – Shrimp – Trout – Tuna

Many cold-water fish are excellent sources of omega-3 fatty acids. They have particularly high concentrations of docosahexaenonic acid (DHA)—the omega-3 that seems to provide the most brain benefits. Studies suggest that increasing your intake of DHA and other omega-3s may provide neuroprotection throughout the lifespan, from the womb to old age. Among other things, omega-3s have been shown to protect brain health in newborns, improve cognitive performance in adults, and prevent or ameliorate age-related cognitive decline. One study even shows that mothers who get enough DHA have smarter kids. Omega-3s also show promise for brain-related diagnoses, including depression and epilepsy. Earlier evidence suggested omega-3s could help in Alzheimer's, but more recent studies challenge that belief.

DHA isn't just good for the brain, it's good for the body, too—studies show many benefits of healthy DHA levels, including a lower risk of cardiovascular disease. Shrimp, salmon, and sardines are also reasonably high in vitamin B12, which has been demonstrated to be one of the most important vitamins for cognitive health and neuroprotection. *References: 8, 24*

Sesame

Lipophilic antioxidants such as those found in sesame seeds and sesame oil are expected to contribute to the prevention of age-related diseases. Sesame seeds are also a good source of the lignans found in flaxseed. *Reference: 25*

Spinach – Kale – Chard

Spinach, kale, chard, and other dark leafy greens are true superfoods, packing in almost 400% of the recommended daily value of vitamin A in just one cup, with healthy doses of vitamin C and E and folic acid as well. Being leafy and dark green, they are also a fantastic source of antioxidants. *References: 2, 4, 6, 10, 14*

Sweet Potatoes

Beta carotene, which gives sweet potatoes their orange color, is a powerful antioxidant. Several studies suggest that a low level of beta carotene (a form of vitamin A) is associated with poorer cognitive function, and that increased intake of beta carotene may protect against cognitive decline in older adulthood. Adding sweet potatoes to your diet is a good idea even independent of its brain benefits—it's high on the list for overall nutrition. *Reference: 26*

Tomatoes

Tomatoes are one of few foods rich in lycopene. Low levels of lycopene have been associate with poor cognitive performance in older people. Lycopene has also been demonstrated as a potential therapeutic for those with Parkinson's disease and diabetes-induced learning and memory impairment. *Reference: 27*

Turmeric

Turmeric is a root that is most commonly sold as a powdered spice. It is bright yellow in color, and is a predominant ingredient in Indian curry powder. Turmeric contains a compound called curcumin, which has been shown to have significant neuroprotective, anti-inflammatory, and anti-Alzheimer's effects. Studies have shown that even relatively infrequent consumption of curcumin may be highly effective in preventing Alzheimer's disease and reducing the physical plaques that accompany the disease. *Reference: 11*

Walnuts

Walnuts have a significant concentration of omega-3 fatty acids. Just 1/4 cup of walnuts has almost 100% of the daily recommended intake of ALA (alpha lineolic acid), one type of omega-3. While the brain benefits of ALA itself are unclear, ALA converts in the body to EPA (Eicosapentaenoic acid), another type of omega-3. Like the DHA in fish, EPA has been shown to have neuroprotective, anti-depressive, and anti-aging properties. *References: 24, 28*

References

1. Frozen fruit pulp of Euterpe oleraceae Mart. (Açaí) prevents hydrogen peroxide-induced damage in the cerebral cortex, cerebellum, and hippocampus of rats. http://bit.ly/ThinkFoodAcai

2. Vitamin E use is associated with improved survival in an Alzheimer's disease cohort. http://bit.ly/ThinkFoodVitaminE1

   Vitamin E and cognitive decline in older persons. http://bit.ly/ThinkFoodVitaminE2

   A Vitamin/nutriceutical formulation improves memory and cognitive performance in community-dwelling adults without dementia. http://bit.ly/ThinkFoodVitaminE3

   Better cognitive performance in elderly taking antioxidant vitamins E and C supplements in combination with nonsteroidal anti-inflammatory drugs: the Cache County Study. http://bit.ly/ThinkFoodVitaminE4

3. Caffeoylquinic acids and flavonoids in the immature inflorescence of globe artichoke, wild cardoon, and cultivated cardoon http://bit.ly/ThinkFoodArtichoke1

   Luteolin promotes long-term potentiation and improves cognitive functions in chronic cerebral hypoperfused rats. http://bit.ly/ThinkFoodArtichoke2

   Luteolin as a therapeutic option for multiple sclerosis. http://bit.ly/ThinkFoodArtichoke3

   Flavonoids, a prenatal prophylaxis via targeting JAK2/STAT3 signaling to oppose IL6/MIA associated autism. http://bit.ly/ThinkFoodArtichoke4

   Luteolin protects dopaminergic neurons from inflammation-induced injury through inhibition of microglial activation. http://bit.ly/ThinkFoodArtichoke5

   Effect of domestic cooking methods on the total antioxidant capacity of vegetables. http://bit.ly/ThinkFoodArtichoke6

4. Significance of vitamin A to brain function, behavior and learning. http://bit.ly/ThinkFoodVitaminA1

   All-trans retinoic acid as a novel therapeutic strategy for Alzheimer's disease. http://bit.ly/ThinkFoodVitaminA2

5. Dietary intake of folate, vitamin B6, vitamin B12 and riboflavin and risk of Parkinson's disease: a case-control study in Japan. http://bit.ly/ThinkFoodVitaminB1

   Long-term association of food and nutrient intakes with cognitive and functional decline: a 13-year follow-up study of elderly French women. http://bit.ly/ThinkFoodVitaminB2

6. Better cognitive performance in elderly taking antioxidant vitamins E and C supplements in combination with nonsteroidal anti-inflammatory drugs: the Cache County Study. http://bit.ly/ThinkFoodVitaminC1

7. Blueberry supplementation improves memory in older adults. http://bit.ly/ThinkFoodBlueberry1

   Grape juice, berries, and walnuts affect brain aging and behavior. http://bit.ly/ThinkFoodBlueberry2

   Blueberry-enriched diet ameliorates age-related declines in NMDA receptor-dependent LTP. http://bit.ly/ThinkFoodBlueberry3

   Effect of a polyphenol-rich wild blueberry extract on cognitive performance of mice, brain antioxidant markers and acetylcholinesterase activity. http://bit.ly/ThinkFoodBlueberry4

   Effects of blackberries on motor and cognitive function in aged rats. http://bit.ly/ThinkFoodBlueberry5

8. Cognitive effects of nutritional deficiency. http://bit.ly/ThinkFoodVitaminB12a

   Long-term association of food and nutrient intakes with cognitive and functional decline: a 13-year follow-up study of elderly French women. http://bit.ly/ThinkFoodVitaminB12b

   Biochemical indicators of vitamin B12 and folate insufficiency and cognitive decline. http://bit.ly/ThinkFoodVitaminB12c

   Efficacy of a vitamin/nutriceutical formulation for moderate-stage to later-stage Alzheimer's disease: a placebo-controlled pilot study. http://bit.ly/ThinkFoodVitaminB12d

9. Cranberries and cranberry products: powerful in vitro, ex vivo, and in vivo sources of antioxidants. http://bit.ly/ThinkFoodCranberry1

   Antioxidant levels of common fruits, vegetables, and juices versus protective activity against in vitro ischemia/reperfusion. http://bit.ly/ThinkFoodCranberry2

10. The hormetic role of dietary antioxidants in free radical-related diseases. http://bit.ly/ThinkFoodAntioxidant1

   Oxidative stress following traumatic brain injury: enhancement of endogenous antioxidant defense systems and the promise of improved outcome. http://bit.ly/ThinkFoodAntioxidant2

11. Naturally occurring phytochemicals for the prevention of Alzheimer's disease. http://bit.ly/ThinkFoodCurcumin1

   Phenolic compounds prevent Alzheimer's pathology through different effects on the amyloid-beta aggregation pathway. http://bit.ly/ThinkFoodCurcumin2

Neuroinflammation in Alzheimer's disease: different molecular targets and potential therapeutic agents including curcumin. http://bit.ly/ThinkFoodCurcumin3

Naturally occurring phytochemicals for the prevention of Alzheimer's disease. http://bit.ly/ThinkFoodCurcumin4

Curcumin as "Curecumin": from kitchen to clinic. http://bit.ly/ThinkFoodCurcumin5

Curcumin improves learning and memory ability and its neuroprotective mechanism in mice. http://bit.ly/ThinkFoodCurcumin6

12. Intake of flavonoid-rich wine, tea, and chocolate by elderly men and women is associated with better cognitive test performance. http://bit.ly/ThinkFoodCocoaFlavanols1

Consumption of cocoa flavanols results in acute improvements in mood and cognitive performance during sustained mental effort. http://bit.ly/ThinkFoodCocoaFlavanols2

Flavonoid intake and cognitive decline over a 10-year period. http://bit.ly/ThinkFoodCocoaFlavanols3

The flavanol (-)-epicatechin prevents stroke damage through the Nrf2/HO1 pathway. http://bit.ly/ThinkFoodCocoaFlavanols4

13. Dietary choline deprivation impairs rat brain mitochondrial function and behavioral phenotype. http://bit.ly/ThinkFoodCholine1

Gene expression profiling of choline-deprived neural precursor cells isolated from mouse brain. http://bit.ly/ThinkFoodCholine2

Perinatal choline influences brain structure and function. http://bit.ly/ThinkFoodCholine3

Hen Egg Phosphatidylcholine in Health; Hen egg phosphatidylcholine combined with vitamin B12 improved memory dysfunction in brain. http://bit.ly/ThinkFoodCholine4

14. A vitamin/nutriceutical formulation improves memory and cognitive performance in community-dwelling adults without dementia. http://bit.ly/ThinkFoodFolicAcid1

Efficacy of a vitamin/nutriceutical formulation for moderate-stage to later-stage Alzheimer's disease: a placebo-controlled pilot study. http://bit.ly/ThinkFoodFolicAcid2

Folate: a key to optimizing health and reducing disease risk in the elderly. http://bit.ly/ThinkFoodFolicAcid3

Folic acid to reduce neonatal mortality from neural tube disorders. http://bit.ly/ThinkFoodFolicAcid4

15. Repeated administration of fresh garlic increases memory retention in rats. http://bit.ly/ThinkFoodGarlic1

Amelioration of early cognitive deficits by aged garlic extract in Alzheimer's transgenic mice. http://bit.ly/ThinkFoodGarlic2

Antioxidative activity and ameliorative effects of memory impairment of sulfur-containing compounds in Allium species. http://bit.ly/ThinkFoodGarlic3

Multiplicity of garlic health effects and Alzheimer's disease. http://bit.ly/ThinkFoodGarlic4

16. Comparison of the antioxidant activities of nine different fruits in human plasma. http://bit.ly/ThinkFoodKiwifruit1

Kiwifruit protects against oxidative DNA damage in human cells and in vitro. http://bit.ly/ThinkFoodKiwifruit2

Cancer prevention and therapy with kiwifruit in Chinese folklore medicine: a study of kiwifruit extracts. http://bit.ly/ThinkFoodKiwifruit3

Identification and Assessment of Antioxidant Capacity of Phytochemicals from Kiwi Fruits. http://bit.ly/ThinkFoodKiwifruit4

17. Dietary niacin and the risk of incident Alzheimer's disease and of cognitive decline http://bit.ly/ThinkFoodNiacin1

Cognitive effects of nutritional deficiency. http://bit.ly/ThinkFoodNiacin2

18. Antioxidant activity of olive polyphenols in humans: a review. http://bit.ly/ThinkFoodPolyphenols1

Neuronutrition and Alzheimer's disease. http://bit.ly/ThinkFoodPolyphenols2

Role of Dietary Polyphenols in Attenuating Brain Edema and Cell Swelling in Cerebral Ischemia. http://bit.ly/ThinkFoodPolyphenols3

Nutrition, brain aging, and neurodegeneration. http://bit.ly/ThinkFoodPolyphenols4

Effectiveness of the Mediterranean diet: can it help delay or prevent Alzheimer's disease? http://bit.ly/ThinkFoodPolyphenols5

Biological activities of phenolic compounds present in virgin olive oil. http://bit.ly/ThinkFoodPolyphenols6

19. Neuroprotective effects of onion extract and quercetin against ischemic neuronal damage in the gerbil hippocampus. http://bit.ly/ThinkFoodQuercetin1

Antidepressant-like effect of onion (Allium cepa L.) powder in a rat behavioral model of depression. http://bit.ly/ThinkFoodQuercetin2

Neuroprotective effect of methanolic extracts of Allium cepa on ischemia and reperfusion-induced cerebral injury. http://bit.ly/ThinkFoodQuercetin3

Onion flesh and onion peel enhance antioxidant status in aged rats. http://bit.ly/ThinkFoodQuercetin4

Antioxidative activity and ameliorative effects of memory impairment of sulfur-containing compounds in Allium species. http://bit.ly/ThinkFoodQuercetin5

20. Intervention of antioxidant system function of aged rats by giving fruit juices with different antioxidant capacities. http://bit.ly/ThinkFoodPomegranate1

Pomegranate juice is potentially better than apple juice in improving antioxidant function in elderly subjects. http://bit.ly/ThinkFoodPomegranate2

Maternal dietary supplementation with pomegranate juice is neuroprotective in an animal model of neonatal hypoxic-ischemic brain injury. http://bit.ly/ThinkFoodPomegranate3

Pomegranate juice decreases amyloid load and improves behavior in a mouse model of Alzheimer's disease. http://bit.ly/ThinkFoodPomegranate4

Pomegranate polyphenols and resveratrol protect the neonatal brain against hypoxic-ischemic injury. http://bit.ly/ThinkFoodPomegranate5

Therapeutic applications of pomegranate (Punica granatum L.): a review. http://bit.ly/ThinkFoodPomegranate6

21. Lysine fortification reduces anxiety and lessens stress in family members in economically weak communities in Northwest Syria. http://bit.ly/ThinkFoodLysine1

Subchronic treatment with amino acid mixture of L-lysine and L-arginine modifies neuroendocrine activation during psychosocial stress in subjects with high trait anxiety. http://bit.ly/ThinkFoodLysine2

Oral treatment with L-lysine and L-arginine reduces anxiety and basal cortisol levels in healthy humans. http://bit.ly/ThinkFoodLysine3

Dietary L-lysine deficiency increases stress-induced anxiety and fecal excretion in rats. http://bit.ly/ThinkFoodLysine4

Prolonged treatment with L-lysine and L-arginine reduces stress-induced anxiety in an elevated plus maze. http://bit.ly/ThinkFoodLysine5

A diet fortified with L-lysine and L-arginine reduces plasma cortisol and blocks anxiogenic response to transportation in pigs. http://bit.ly/ThinkFoodLysine6

22. Magnesium sulfate reduces inflammation-associated brain injury in fetal mice. http://bit.ly/ThinkFoodMagnesium1

Magnesium and posthypoxic changes of nitrergic population in rat hippocampus. http://bit.ly/ThinkFoodMagnesium2

Prophylactic intravenous magnesium sulfate for treatment of aneurysmal subarachnoid hemorrhage: a randomized, placebo-controlled, clinical study. http://bit.ly/ThinkFoodMagnesium3

23. An extract of Salvia (sage) with anticholinesterase properties improves memory and attention in healthy older volunteers. http://bit.ly/ThinkFoodSage1

The pharmacological effects of Salvia species on the central nervous system. http://bit.ly/ThinkFoodSage2

Effects of Salvia officinalis L. (sage) leaves on memory retention and its interaction with the cholinergic system in rats. http://bit.ly/ThinkFoodSage3

Medicinal plants and Alzheimer's disease: Integrating ethnobotanical and contemporary scientific evidence. http://bit.ly/ThinkFoodSage4

Salvia lavandulaefolia (Spanish sage) enhances memory in healthy young volunteers. http://bit.ly/ThinkFoodSage5

Positive modulation of mood and cognitive performance following administration of acute doses of Salvia lavandulaefolia essential oil to healthy young volunteers. http://bit.ly/ThinkFoodSage6

24. Cognitive and cardiovascular benefits of docosahexaenoic acid in aging and cognitive decline. http://bit.ly/ThinkFoodDHA1

Omega-3 fatty acids: potential role in the management of early Alzheimer's disease. http://bit.ly/ThinkFoodDHA2

Effects of long-chain polyunsaturated fatty acid supplementation on neurodevelopment in childhood: a review of human studies. http://bit.ly/ThinkFoodDHA3

DHA may prevent age-related dementia. http://bit.ly/ThinkFoodDHA4

Docosahexaenoic acid supplementation increases prefrontal cortex activation during sustained attention in healthy boys: a placebo-controlled, dose-ranging, functional magnetic resonance imaging study. http://bit.ly/ThinkFoodDHA5

PUFA for prevention and treatment of dementia? http://bit.ly/ThinkFoodDHA6

Qualitative analysis of hippocampal plastic changes in rats with epilepsy supplemented with oral omega-3 fatty acids. http://bit.ly/ThinkFoodDHA7

Maternal docosahexaenoic acid-enriched diet prevents neonatal brain injury. http://bit.ly/ThinkFoodDHA8

Omega-3 polyunsaturated fatty acids and depression: a review of the evidence. http://bit.ly/ThinkFoodDHA9

Serum phospholipid docosahexaenonic acid is associated with cognitive functioning during middle adulthood. http://bit.ly/ThinkFoodDHA10

Maternal supplementation with very-long-chain n-3 fatty acids during pregnancy and lactation augments children's IQ at 4 years of age. http://bit.ly/ThinkFoodDHA11

Essential fatty acids and the brain. http://bit.ly/ThinkFoodDHA12

Omega-3 fatty acids reverse age-related decreases in nuclear receptors and increase neurogenesis in old rats. http://bit.ly/ThinkFoodDHA13

Effects of long-chain polyunsaturated fatty acid supplementation on neurodevelopment in childhood: a review of human studies. http://bit.ly/ThinkFoodDHA14

Omega-3 polyunsaturated fatty acids and human health outcomes. http://bit.ly/ThinkFoodDHA15

Omega-3 polyunsaturated fatty acids and depression: a review of the evidence. http://bit.ly/ThinkFoodDHA16

25. Analysis of antioxidant activities in vegetable oils and fat soluble vitamins and biofactors by the PAO-SO method. http://bit.ly/ThinkFoodSesame

26. A randomized trial of beta carotene supplementation and cognitive function in men: the Physicians' Health Study II. http://bit.ly/ThinkFoodBetaCarotene1

Association between serum beta-carotene levels and decline of cognitive function in high-functioning older persons with or without apolipoprotein E 4 alleles: MacArthur studies of successful aging. http://bit.ly/ThinkFoodBetaCarotene2

Nutritional biomarkers in Alzheimer's disease: the association between carotenoids, n-3 fatty acids, and dementia severity. http://bit.ly/ThinkFoodBetaCarotene3

27. Gene expression profiling of choline-deprived neural precursor cells isolated from mouse brain. http://bit.ly/ThinkFoodLycopene1

Perinatal choline influences brain structure and function. http://bit.ly/ThinkFoodLycopene2

Plasma carotenoid levels and cognitive performance in an elderly population: results of the EVA Study. http://bit.ly/ThinkFoodLycopene3

Lycopene attenuates diabetes-associated cognitive decline in rats. http://bit.ly/ThinkFoodLycopene4

Intake of tomato-enriched diet protects from 6-hydroxydopamine-induced degeneration of rat nigral dopaminergic neurons. http://bit.ly/ThinkFoodLycopene5

28. Grape juice, berries, and walnuts affect brain aging and behavior. http://bit.ly/ThinkFoodWalnuts

29. Effect of breakfast composition on cognitive processes in elementary school children. http://bit.ly/ThinkFoodOats1

Selenoproteins and the aging brain. http://bit.ly/ThinkFoodOats2

Protective effects of selenium on fluoride induced alterations in certain enzymes in brain of mice. http://bit.ly/ThinkFoodOats3

The neuroprotective functions of selenoprotein M and its role in cytosolic calcium regulation. http://bit.ly/ThinkFoodOats4

30. Higher dietary intake of lignans is associated with better cognitive performance in postmenopausal women. http://bit.ly/ThinkFoodFlaxseed1

Dietary phytoestrogen intake and cognitive function in older women. http://bit.ly/ThinkFoodFlaxseed2

Pilot evaluation of flaxseed for the management of hot flashes. http://bit.ly/ThinkFoodFlaxseed3

A special thank you to all of the contributing bloggers, chef-proprietor Dorothée Mitrani-Bell and chef Denise Ravizza of La Note Restaurant in Berkeley California, photographer and designer Jason Whalen from Agency Charlie, Cassie Kovacevich from Open-First, and the Posit Science team. Without all of you, this book would not be possible.